Wealthyfull

The Science of Building Financial Freedom

Dr. R Senthil MBA.,Ph.D.,CFP.,AIII

Chennai • Bangalore

CLEVER FOX PUBLISHING
Chennai, India

Published by CLEVER FOX PUBLISHING 2023
Copyright © Dr. R Senthil MBA.,Ph.D.,CFP.,AIII 2023

All Rights Reserved.
ISBN: 978-93-56484-07-8

CONTENTS

AUTHOR SELF-INTRODUCTION

Greetings,

I am Dr. R. Senthil, the proud author of "Wealthyfull: The Science of Building Financial Freedom." In this comprehensive guide, I provide practical steps and strategies to help you achieve true financial independence.

"Wealthyfull" serves as a roadmap for your financial journey. I cover various aspects such as budgeting, investment options, and wealth accumulation, offering practical insights and expert advice for informed decisions and financial control.

I also emphasize the importance of giving back for a prosperous and equitable world. Throughout the book, you'll find practical examples, case studies, and actionable advice to facilitate remarkable transformation.

Thank you for choosing "Wealthyfull" as your guide to unlock the science of financial freedom and pave the way to prosperity.

Warm regards,
Dr. R. Senthil

CHAPTER 1

INTRODUCTION

Have you ever dreamed of financial freedom? The kind of freedom that allows you to live life on your own terms, without the constant worry of money holding you back? If you're like most people, the answer is a resounding yes. But unfortunately, for many, financial freedom remains just a dream.

Maybe you've tried to achieve financial freedom before but felt overwhelmed by the amount of conflicting advice out there. Or maybe you simply don't know where to start. Whatever your situation, I'm here to tell you that achieving financial freedom is not only possible, but it's also within your reach. And in this book, I'm going to show you how.

Before we dive into the strategies and techniques that will help you build wealth and achieve financial freedom, let's take a step back and consider why financial freedom is so important. We all know that money can't buy happiness, but it can certainly make life a lot easier. Financial freedom means that you can afford to pursue your passions, take care of your loved ones, and live life on your own terms. It means that you don't have to worry about living paycheck to paycheck, or stress about how you'll pay for unexpected expenses. And it means that you have the freedom to make choices that align with your values, rather than simply doing what pays the bills.

But here's the thing: achieving financial freedom isn't just about earning more money. It's about developing the right mindset, adopting smart habits, and making informed decisions about how to manage your money. And that's where this book comes in.

In the following chapters, we'll explore the science of building financial freedom, covering everything from creating a financial plan, to budgeting, investing, building passive income, and more. You'll learn practical strategies and techniques for managing your money, and for making it work for you. And most importantly, you'll learn how to adopt a wealth mindset that will help you achieve your financial goals and live the life you've always dreamed of.

So, are you ready to take control of your financial future? Let's get started.

Backround

Financial freedom is a goal that many people strive for, but unfortunately, it's one that few achieve. At its core, financial freedom means having the financial resources to live the life you want, without being limited by money. It means having the ability to pursue your passions, take risks, and make choices based on what truly matters to you, rather than being forced to make decisions based on financial constraints.

For many people, achieving financial freedom is an important step towards overall happiness and well-being. When we're not worried about money, we can focus on the things that truly matter, like spending time with loved ones, pursuing our hobbies, and contributing to the causes we care about. Financial freedom can also reduce stress and anxiety, as we don't have to constantly worry about bills, debt, and unexpected expenses.

But financial freedom isn't just about personal happiness and well-being. It can also have broader social and economic impacts.

When people have more financial freedom, they're more likely to take risks and start their own businesses, which can create jobs and drive economic growth. They're also more likely to give back to their communities, through charitable donations or volunteering. In short, financial freedom can have a ripple effect that benefits not just the individual, but also society as a whole.

Unfortunately, achieving financial freedom is often easier said than done. In today's world, it can be tough to make ends meet, let alone save for the future. Many people struggle with debt, low wages, and a lack of financial literacy. But the good news is that achieving financial freedom is possible, no matter your current financial situation. By developing the right mindset, adopting smart habits, and learning how to manage your money effectively, you can build wealth and achieve the financial freedom you deserve. And that's exactly what this book is all about.

The book is divided into three main parts, each of which is designed to help you build your financial freedom from the ground up. we'll focus on the foundational principles of wealth creation, such as setting goals, creating a budget, and managing debt. We'll explore the psychology of money and help you develop a money mindset that will set you up for success.

We'll dive deeper into the mechanics of building wealth. We'll cover topics such as investing, saving for retirement, and building passive income streams. You'll learn how to make your money work for you, rather than the other way around.

Finally, we'll help you take your financial freedom to the next level. We'll explore advanced strategies for building wealth and achieving financial independence, such as real estate investing, entrepreneurship, and portfolio diversification. You'll learn how to create a wealth-building plan that's tailored to your individual goals and circumstances.

Throughout the book, you'll find practical exercises, case studies, and examples that will help you apply the concepts to your own life. Whether you're just starting out on your financial journey, or you're looking to take your wealth to the next level, this book will provide you with the tools and knowledge you need to achieve financial freedom and build the life you want.

The Science of Building Financial Freedom" apart from other personal finance books on the market is our unique approach to building wealth. We don't just provide you with a set of generic tips and tricks for saving money or investing in stocks. Instead, we take a holistic approach to wealth creation that focuses on building a solid financial foundation, developing the right mindset, and leveraging advanced strategies to grow your wealth over time.

One of the key advantages of our approach is that it's highly adaptable to your individual circumstances. Whether you're a college student just starting out on your financial journey, or a seasoned investor looking to diversify your portfolio, our book provides a roadmap for building financial freedom that can be customized to your specific goals and needs.

Another key advantage of our book is our focus on the science of wealth creation. We take a data-driven approach to personal finance, drawing on the latest research and insights from the field of behavioral economics to help you make the most informed decisions possible. You'll learn not just what to do to build wealth, but why it works, and how to apply these insights to your own life.

Finally, our book is highly practical and actionable. We don't just give you theoretical concepts to ponder; we provide you with concrete tools and exercises that will help you put these concepts into practice in your own life. Whether you're looking to build a budget, create a passive income stream, or invest in real estate, our book provides step-by-step guidance that will help you achieve your financial goals.

Overall, if you're looking for a comprehensive, science-backed, and highly actionable guide to building financial freedom, "Wealthyfull" is the book for you.

Call to action: Encourage readers to continue reading and to take action towards achieving financial freedom.

Now that you've learned about the importance of financial freedom and what you can expect from this book, it's time to take action. Building wealth isn't easy, and it won't happen overnight, but it's an achievable goal if you're willing to put in the effort and follow the right steps.

Throughout this book, you'll learn about the foundational principles of wealth creation, including budgeting, saving, investing, and more. You'll also gain insights into the psychology of money, and how your mindset can impact your financial success.

But learning is only the first step. To truly achieve financial freedom, you must be willing to take action. That means setting clear financial goals, creating a plan for achieving them and taking consistent, deliberate action towards those goals. It means being disciplined with your spending and making smart investments that will grow your wealth over time. And it means developing a mindset that's focused on long-term success, rather than short-term gratification.

Use the insights and strategies in this book to guide your decisions, and take deliberate action towards building your wealth over time. And most importantly, stay committed to the journey, even when it gets challenging.

Remember, financial freedom is not just a destination, it's a journey. And with the right mindset, tools, and strategies, you can achieve it. So, let's get started!

CHAPTER 2

MINDSET MATTERS

HAPPY

Mindset Matters:

When it comes to building wealth and achieving financial freedom, mindset matters just as much as any other factor. Our thoughts and beliefs around money can have a significant impact on our ability to achieve our financial goals.

Many of us hold limiting beliefs around money that have been ingrained in us since childhood. Perhaps we were told that the pursuit of wealth is selfish and greedy, or that money is the root of all evil. Whatever the case may be, these beliefs can hold us back from achieving our full potential when it comes to building wealth.

In order to adopt a wealth mindset, it's important to first identify and challenge any limiting beliefs we may hold about money. This can be a difficult and uncomfortable process, but it's an essential step towards achieving financial freedom.

One common limiting belief around money is the idea that it's somehow inherently bad or immoral. This belief can manifest in a variety of ways, such as feeling guilty or ashamed about wanting to make money, or avoiding opportunities for financial growth because they conflict with our values.

To challenge this belief, it's important to reframe our thinking around money. Money is simply a tool that can be used for good or bad purposes, depending on how it's used. By adopting a mindset that sees money as a positive force for change, we can begin to see opportunities for financial growth in a new light.

Another common limiting belief is the idea that we are not capable of achieving financial success. This belief can stem from a variety of sources, such as past failures or negative feedback from others. To challenge this belief, it's important to focus on our strengths and past successes and to surround ourselves with supportive and positive influences.

By adopting a wealth mindset and challenging limiting beliefs around money, we can open ourselves up to new opportunities and achieve our financial goals. In the next section of this book, we'll provide practical strategies for adopting a wealth mindset in your own life.

The Power of Mindset:

The power of mindset cannot be overstated when it comes to building wealth. Our thoughts and beliefs around money can have a profound impact on our financial decisions and outcomes. There are two main mindsets when it comes to money: scarcity and abundance.

A scarcity mindset is one in which we believe that there is a limited amount of money and resources available. This mindset can lead to feelings of fear, anxiety, and lack. We may feel that we need to hold onto every penny and not take any risks, for fear of losing what we have. This can result in missed opportunities for growth and financial success.

On the other hand, an abundance mindset is one in which we believe that there is more than enough money and resources available to us. This mindset can lead to feelings of confidence, optimism, and abundance. We may be more willing to take risks and pursue opportunities for growth and financial success.

Our mindset can impact our financial success in many ways. For example, if we believe that there is a limited amount of money available, we may be more likely to focus on saving and cutting expenses rather than investing and growing our wealth. This can lead to a slower rate of financial growth over time. Conversely, if we believe that there is an abundance of money available, we may be more willing to take risks and invest in opportunities that have the potential for greater financial returns.

In the next section, we will explore some common limiting beliefs around money and how they can impact our financial success. By becoming aware of these beliefs and challenging them, we can begin to shift our mindset towards abundance and increase our potential for financial success.

An abundance mindset, on the other hand, is characterized by a belief in the unlimited potential of the universe and a sense of abundance and prosperity. Those who hold an abundance mindset are more likely to believe that there are always opportunities for growth and success and that they have the power to create wealth and abundance in their lives.

Having an abundance mindset can lead to a more positive outlook on life, as well as increased motivation and confidence in pursuing financial goals. For example, someone with an abundance mindset may be more likely to start a business or invest in stocks because they believe that there is unlimited potential for growth and success.

In contrast, a scarcity mindset can hold us back from pursuing opportunities and taking risks that could lead to financial success. If we believe that there is a limited amount of wealth and resources available, we may feel like there is no point in trying to achieve financial freedom because it's unattainable.

Therefore, it's important to recognize and challenge any limiting beliefs we may have around money and to adopt an abundance mindset in order to achieve financial freedom. By doing so, we open ourselves up to greater opportunities and possibilities for creating wealth and abundance in our lives.

Remember this Five Key Points

1. Mindset is a crucial factor in building wealth and achieving financial freedom.
2. A scarcity mindset is characterized by a belief in limited resources and a sense of lack, while an abundance mindset is characterized by a belief in unlimited potential and prosperity.
3. Holding an abundance mindset can lead to a more positive outlook, increased motivation, and confidence in pursuing financial goals.
4. A scarcity mindset can hold us back from pursuing opportunities and taking risks that could lead to financial success.
5. Challenging limiting beliefs around money and adopting an abundance mindset is important for creating greater opportunities and possibilities for creating wealth and abundance in our lives.

Limiting Beliefs:

Challenging Limiting Beliefs:

Now that we have identified some common limiting beliefs around money and wealth, let's explore how to challenge and overcome them. One effective strategy is to examine the evidence that supports or refutes our beliefs. For example, if we believe that money is evil, we can ask ourselves if that belief is true for all cases. Are there people who have used money for good and positive causes? What about the positive impact that having more money can have on our lives and the lives of those around us?

Another strategy is to reframe our limiting beliefs into more empowering beliefs. Instead of "money is evil," we can reframe it as "money is a tool that can be used for good or bad, and I choose to use it for good." This helps to shift our mindset from a scarcity mentality to an abundance mentality, where we see money as a resource that we can use to create more abundance and opportunity in our lives.

Lastly, seeking out positive role models and mentors can be a powerful way to challenge and overcome limiting beliefs. Surrounding ourselves with people who have achieved financial success in a positive and ethical way can help us to reframe our beliefs and see new possibilities for our own financial future.

By challenging and overcoming our limiting beliefs around money and wealth, we can create a more positive and empowering mindset that will help us to achieve financial freedom and build the life we truly desire.

Adopting a Wealth Mindset:

Having a wealth mindset means having a positive attitude towards money and abundance. It means believing that wealth is possible for everyone, including yourself, and that you are capable of achieving financial freedom. Adopting a wealth mindset requires a shift in our thoughts and beliefs around money, and it can be a powerful tool in building long-term wealth.

One effective strategy for adopting a wealth mindset is through the use of positive affirmations. Positive affirmations are statements that you repeat to yourself to reinforce positive beliefs and attitudes. For example, you might say, "I am worthy of wealth and abundance" or "Money flows easily and effortlessly to me." By repeating these affirmations daily, you can begin to shift your thoughts and beliefs around money towards a more positive and abundance-focused mindset.

Visualization is another powerful technique for adopting a wealth mindset. This involves creating mental images of yourself achieving your financial goals and experiencing the lifestyle that comes with financial freedom. By visualizing yourself as already having achieved your goals, you begin to shift your mindset towards a state of abundance and wealth. Visualization can be done through guided meditations, vision boards, or simply by taking a few minutes each day to visualize your desired outcomes.

Gratitude practices are also effective in developing a wealth mindset. By focusing on what you already have and expressing gratitude for it, you begin to shift your mindset towards abundance and attract more positivity and abundance into your life. This can be as simple as writing down three things you are grateful for each day or expressing gratitude before meals.

Developing a growth mindset is also crucial in adopting a wealth mindset. A growth mindset is a belief that you can always improve and grow, and that challenges and failures are opportunities for growth and learning. By embracing challenges and using them as opportunities for growth, you can develop a mindset that is focused on progress and success.

Adopting a wealth mindset is not an overnight process, but with consistent practice, it is possible to transform your mindset and achieve financial freedom. In the next section, we will examine the practical steps you can take towards building wealth and achieving financial freedom.

The Role of Habits in Building Wealth:

When it comes to achieving financial freedom, adopting a wealth mindset is crucial, but it's not enough. To turn mindset into action, it's essential to develop healthy financial habits. Habits are powerful because they are automatic and require minimal effort once they're established. This makes them a powerful tool for building wealth, as they allow us to make consistent progress towards our financial goals without relying solely on willpower or motivation.

One of the most important financial habits to develop is budgeting. Budgeting involves creating a plan for how you will allocate your income and expenses, with the goal of ensuring that you are living within your means and saving money for the future.

Budgeting can be challenging at first, but there are many tools and resources available to help you get started. For example, you can use a budgeting app like Mint or You Need a Budget (YNAB) to track your expenses and create a budget that works for you.

Another essential financial habit is saving. Saving is the foundation of building wealth, as it allows you to accumulate resources over time and invest them in opportunities that can generate even more wealth. To make saving a habit, it's important to automate the process as much as possible. This can involve setting up automatic transfers from your checking account to a savings account or using a savings app that rounds up your purchases and puts the spare change into savings.

Investing is another critical financial habit to develop. Investing involves putting your money to work in assets that have the potential to generate a return over time, such as stocks, bonds, or real estate. Investing can be intimidating for beginners, but there are many resources available to help you get started. It's important to remember that investing is a long-term strategy, and success requires patience, discipline, and a willingness to take calculated risks.

In conclusion, developing healthy financial habits is essential for building wealth and achieving financial freedom. Budgeting, saving, and investing are three key habits to develop, but there are many other habits that can also contribute to your financial success. By making these habits a part of your daily routine, you can build a solid foundation for your financial future.

Practical Tips for Developing Financial Habits

Developing healthy financial habits can be challenging, especially if you are used to living paycheck to paycheck or have a lot of debt. However, with some practical tips and a little bit of discipline, anyone can develop habits that will set them on the path to financial freedom.

One strategy for developing healthy financial habits is to automate your savings. This means setting up automatic transfers from your checking account to your savings account on a regular basis. This can help you build up your emergency fund, save for a down payment on a home, or invest for retirement without having to think about it too much.

Another strategy is to use a budgeting app or tool to help you track your spending and stay on top of your finances. There are many great options available, including Mint, YNAB (You Need a Budget), and Personal Capital. These tools can help you identify areas where you may be overspending and make adjustments to your budget accordingly.

Finally, it's important to prioritize your spending and focus on the things that truly matter to you. This may mean cutting back on certain expenses, such as eating out or buying new clothes, in order to save for a bigger goal, such as a dream vacation or early retirement. By being intentional about your spending and focusing on the things that truly bring you joy, you can develop healthy financial habits that will help you achieve your financial goals.

Overall, developing healthy financial habits is an essential part of adopting a wealth mindset and achieving financial freedom. By automating your savings, using a budgeting app, and prioritizing your spending, you can set yourself up for long-term financial success.

Mindset and Relationships:

When it comes to achieving financial freedom, our mindset can have a profound impact on our relationships, both personal and professional. If we surround ourselves with people who have a negative or limiting mindset, it can be difficult to maintain the positive outlook and motivation needed to succeed in our financial goals.

On the other hand, building relationships with individuals who share our values and goals can be incredibly empowering. These individuals can provide support, encouragement, and even new ideas or opportunities that can help us achieve financial success.

It's important to remember that relationships are a two-way street, and that we also have a responsibility to be a positive influence on others. By adopting a wealth mindset and striving for financial freedom, we can inspire and motivate those around us to do the same.

However, there may be relationships in our lives that are holding us back or contributing to a negative mindset. It's important to evaluate these relationships and determine whether they are truly serving our best interests. Setting boundaries and limiting our exposure to negative influences can be difficult, but it's a necessary step towards achieving financial success and building healthy relationships.

In the next sections, we will discuss practical strategies for surrounding ourselves with positive and supportive individuals, setting boundaries in our relationships, and managing difficult situations that may arise.

The impact of mindset on our relationships extends beyond personal connections to our professional lives as well. Our mindset can affect our ability to negotiate, network, and take risks, all of which are essential for building a successful career and achieving financial freedom.

For example, someone with a scarcity mindset may be hesitant to negotiate their salary or ask for a raise, fearing rejection or believing that they don't deserve more money. On the other hand, someone with an abundance mindset may see negotiations as an opportunity to create value and build stronger relationships with their employer.

Similarly, our mindset can affect our ability to network effectively. Those with a scarcity mindset may view networking as a transactional activity, solely focused on what they can gain from others. In contrast, those with an abundance mindset approach networking as an opportunity to build mutually beneficial relationships and contribute value to others.

To develop a wealth mindset in our professional lives, it's important to practice positive self-talk, focus on building genuine connections, and take calculated risks that align with our values and goals. By doing so, we can create a supportive network and opportunities for growth and advancement in our careers.

In conclusion, our mindset can have a significant impact on our relationships, both personal and professional. By adopting a wealth mindset, we can attract and surround ourselves with positive and supportive individuals who share our goals and values. It's important to set boundaries and manage relationships that may be holding us back, whether it's with family, friends, or colleagues. Remember that our relationships can impact our financial success, so it's crucial to cultivate healthy and supportive connections in our personal and professional lives.

Overcoming Setbacks:

The road to financial freedom is not always smooth sailing. Despite our best efforts, setbacks and obstacles can arise that threaten to derail our progress. However, it is important to recognize that setbacks are a natural part of the journey and can be opportunities for growth and learning.

One of the keys to overcoming setbacks is to reframe our mindset around failure. Rather than seeing failure as a negative outcome, we can choose to view it as an opportunity for growth and learning. By reframing our perspective, we can use setbacks as a chance to identify what went wrong and develop new strategies for moving forward.

Another important strategy for overcoming setbacks is seeking support from others. This can include working with a mentor or coach who has experience in our desired financial area or seeking advice from friends and family members who have achieved financial success. Having a support system in place can help us stay motivated and provide us with the guidance and encouragement we need to keep going.

Staying committed to our goals is also crucial when it comes to overcoming setbacks. It can be easy to get discouraged when things don't go according to plan, but it is important to remember why we started on this journey in the first place. By keeping our goals in mind and staying focused on our desired outcomes, we can push through setbacks and continue making progress towards financial freedom.

Overall, setbacks are an inevitable part of any journey towards financial freedom. However, by reframing our mindset around failure, seeking support from others, and staying committed to our goals, we can overcome setbacks and continue making progress towards the financial future we desire.

Strategies for Overcoming Setbacks

While setbacks can be discouraging, they do not have to derail our journey towards financial freedom. By adopting a growth mindset and using the following strategies, we can overcome setbacks and continue moving forward:

a. **Reframe failures** as opportunities for growth - Rather than viewing setbacks as a reflection of our abilities or worth, we can choose to see them as opportunities to learn and improve. By reframing failures as part of the learning process, we can stay motivated and focused on our goals.

b. **Seek support from a mentor or coach** - Having a mentor or coach can provide valuable guidance and support during difficult times. They can offer a fresh perspective, help us identify areas for improvement, and hold us accountable for our goals.

c. **Stay committed to our goals** - Setbacks can be a test of our commitment to our goals. By staying focused on our long-term vision and reminding ourselves of why we started on this journey, we can stay motivated and committed to achieving financial freedom.

d. **Practice self-care** - Setbacks can be stressful and emotionally draining, so it's important to prioritize self-care. This can include activities such as exercise, meditation, or spending time with loved ones.

e. **Learn from past mistakes** - Setbacks can also provide an opportunity to reflect on past mistakes and identify areas for improvement. By taking the time to analyze what went wrong and how we can do better in the future, we can turn setbacks into valuable learning experiences.

By using these strategies, we can overcome setbacks and continue making progress towards our financial goals. Remember, setbacks are a natural part of the journey towards financial freedom, but they do not have to define our success.

Conclusion:

In conclusion, the first chapter of this book has emphasized the importance of adopting a wealth mindset as a powerful tool for building wealth and achieving financial freedom. We have discussed the difference between a scarcity mindset and an abundance mindset and how each can impact our financial decisions and outcomes. Additionally, we have examined common limiting beliefs around money and wealth and provided strategies for identifying and challenging these beliefs.

We have also discussed the role of habits in developing a wealth mindset and provided practical tips for developing healthy financial habits. Furthermore, we have examined the impact of our mindset on our relationships, both personal and professional, and provided strategies for setting boundaries and managing relationships that may be holding us back.

Lastly, we have discussed the inevitable setbacks that may occur on the journey to achieving financial freedom and provided strategies for overcoming these setbacks. It is important to reframe failures as opportunities for growth, seek support from a mentor or coach, and stay committed to our goals.

It is my hope that this chapter has encouraged readers to take action towards adopting a wealth mindset and has provided practical strategies for doing so. With the right mindset, habits, and support system, anyone can achieve financial freedom.

CHAPTER-3

CREATING
A FINANCIAL PLAN

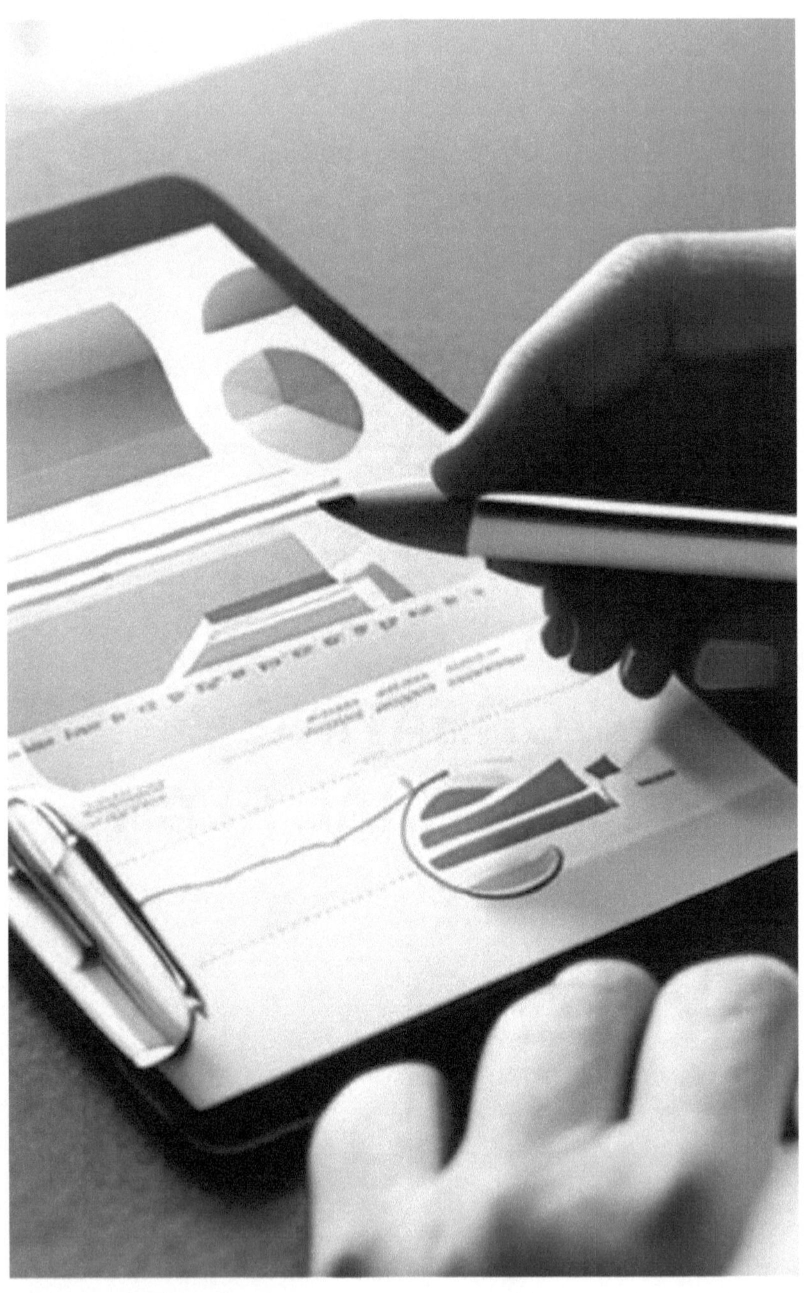

I Introduction

Creating a solid financial plan is an essential step towards achieving financial security and stability. A financial plan is a comprehensive document that outlines an individual's current financial situation, financial goals, and strategies for achieving those goals. It is a roadmap that helps individuals prioritize their spending, manage debt, save for the future, and invest wisely.

A financial plan is not a one-time activity but rather a continuous process that requires regular review and revision. It is crucial to create a financial plan that aligns with one's values and goals to achieve financial success. In this section, we will discuss the importance of creating a financial plan and what it entails.

II The Importance of Creating a Financial Plan

A. Understanding Your Current Financial Situation

The first step in creating a financial plan is to assess your current financial situation. This includes evaluating your income, expenses, debts, assets, and liabilities. Once you have a clear understanding of your financial situation, you can develop strategies for managing your money more effectively and make informed decisions about how to allocate your resources.

B. Setting Financial Goals

Financial goals help provide direction and focus in achieving financial stability and success. Setting realistic and achievable financial goals requires careful consideration of both short-term and long-term objectives. This can include saving for retirement, purchasing a home, paying off debt, or building an emergency fund.

C. Developing Strategies for Achieving Your Goals

Once you have established your financial goals, you need to develop a plan of action for achieving them. This may include creating a budget, reducing expenses, increasing your income, investing in stocks or mutual funds, or paying off debt.

D. Managing Risk

Risk management is an essential component of a financial plan. Identifying and managing risk helps to protect your financial resources and ensures that you are prepared for unforeseen circumstances. This can include purchasing insurance, creating an emergency fund, and diversifying investments.

E. Continual Monitoring and Review

Creating a financial plan is not a one-time activity. It is essential to regularly review and monitor your plan to ensure that it remains aligned with your goals and objectives. This can include reviewing your investments, tracking your expenses, and updating your plan as your financial situation and goals change.

III What a Financial Plan Entails

A. Developing a Budget

Creating a budget is a critical component of a financial plan. It helps to track your income and expenses, identify areas where you can reduce spending, and prioritize your financial goals.

B. Establishing an Emergency Fund

An emergency fund is essential in providing a financial safety net in case of unforeseen circumstances. This can include job loss, unexpected medical bills, or home repairs. The emergency fund should be easily accessible, such as a savings account, and ideally should cover three to six months' worth of expenses.

C. Managing Debt

Debt management is a crucial component of a financial plan. It involves developing a plan for paying off debt, prioritizing high-interest debt, and avoiding taking on new debt whenever possible.

D. Saving for Retirement

Saving for retirement is an important long-term financial goal. It involves developing a strategy for investing in retirement accounts, such as a 401(k) or IRA, and determining the amount needed to save to achieve your desired retirement lifestyle.

E. Investing Wisely

Investing in stocks, bonds, or mutual funds is an essential component of a financial plan. It involves creating a diversified investment portfolio that aligns with your risk tolerance, financial goals, and time horizon.

Conclusion

Creating a financial plan is an essential step towards achieving financial stability and success. It requires an understanding of your current financial situation, setting realistic financial goals, developing strategies for achieving those goals, managing risk, and regularly monitoring and reviewing your plan. By taking the time to develop a financial plan that aligns

II Assessing Your Current Financial Situation
Identifying income and expenses
Reviewing debts and liabilities
Calculating net worth

Assessing your current financial situation is a crucial step in creating a comprehensive financial plan. Without a clear understanding of your income, expenses, debts, and liabilities, it's impossible to create a realistic and effective plan that aligns with your goals and values.

The first step in assessing your current financial situation is to identify your income and expenses. This includes all sources of income, such as wages, salaries, bonuses, and investment income, as well as all expenses, such as housing costs, food, transportation, entertainment, and debt payments. To get an accurate picture of your income and expenses, it's important to track your spending over several months and to include both fixed and variable expenses.

Once you've identified your income and expenses, it's time to review your debts and liabilities. This includes credit card debt, student loans, car loans, and mortgages, as well as any other liabilities you may have, such as outstanding medical bills or tax debts. It's important to understand the terms of each debt, including the interest rate, minimum monthly payment, and any fees or penalties for late payments.

Calculating your net worth is the final step in assessing your current financial situation. Your net worth is the difference between your assets and liabilities and provides a snapshot of your overall financial health. To calculate your net worth, add up the value of all your assets, including cash, investments, real estate, and personal property, and subtract your total liabilities. Ideally, your net worth should increase over time as you pay down debt and accumulate assets.

Assessing your current financial situation can be overwhelming, especially if you have significant debt or expenses. However, it's important to remember that the goal of this step is not to judge or criticize yourself but rather to gain a clear understanding of where you are financially so that you can make informed decisions about where you want to go.

In addition to providing a baseline for creating a financial plan, assessing your current financial situation can also be a valuable tool for identifying areas where you can cut costs or increase income. For example, if you discover that you're spending more on dining out than you realized, you may decide to eat at home more often or find ways to save money on groceries.

Overall, assessing your current financial situation is an essential step in creating a financial plan that aligns with your goals and values. By taking the time to identify your income and expenses, review your debts and liabilities, and calculate your net worth, you can gain a clear understanding of where you stand financially and make informed decisions about how to move forward.

Here are some examples to illustrate the process of assessing your current financial situation:

1. Identifying Income and Expenses:
Start by gathering all your financial documents and make a list of your income sources, including your salary, bonuses, commissions, and any other sources of income. Then, make a

list of all your expenses, including fixed expenses such as rent/ mortgage payments, utility bills, car payments, insurance, and variable expenses such as groceries, entertainment, and clothing.

For instance, if your monthly income is $5,000 and the amount of your monthly expenses to $4,500, then you have a monthly surplus of $500.

2. Reviewing Debts and Liabilities:

Make a list of all your debts and liabilities, including credit card debts, student loans, car loans, and any other debts you owe. Identify the interest rates, the minimum monthly payments, and the total amount owed for each debt.

For example, if you owe $10,000 in credit card debt with an interest rate of 18%, and you make the minimum monthly payment of $200, it will take you more than 10 years to pay off the debt and you will end up paying over $10,000 in interest.

3. Calculating Net Worth:

To calculate your net worth, subtract your total liabilities from your total assets. Assets can include savings accounts, investments, retirement accounts, real estate, and other valuable possessions.

For instance, if your total assets are worth $250,000 and your total liabilities are $150,000, your net worth is $100,000.

By assessing your current financial situation, you can gain a better understanding of your income, expenses, debts, and net worth, which can help you create a realistic financial plan that aligns with your goals and values.

III Setting Financial Goals

Creating a financial plan is essentially about setting financial goals and taking action to achieve them. Without goals, it is difficult to know where to focus our efforts or measure progress. In this section, we will discuss how to set financial goals that are specific, measurable, achievable, relevant, and time-bound (SMART).

Short-term vs. Long-term Goals

1. One of the first steps in setting financial goals is to distinguish between short-term and long-term goals. Short-term goals are those that we want to achieve within the next year or two, while long-term goals are those that we want to achieve over a longer period of time, such as five or ten years. Both types of goals are important, and it is important to have a balance between them. Short-term goals help us stay motivated and see progress quickly, while long-term goals provide direction and focus.

SMART Goal-Setting Principles

2. Once we have distinguished between short-term and long-term goals, it is important to apply the SMART goal-setting principles. SMART stands for Specific, Measurable, Achievable, Relevant, and Time-bound. Specific goals are clear and well-defined, so we know exactly what we are working towards. Measurable goals are those that we can quantify, so we can track progress and know when we have achieved them. Achievable goals are those that are challenging but realistic, so we do not become discouraged.

Relevant goals are those that are aligned with our values and priorities, so we are motivated to achieve them. Time-bound goals are those that have a specific deadline, so we are accountable and can stay on track.

Prioritizing Goals based on Importance and Feasibility

3. After setting specific, measurable, achievable, relevant, and time-bound goals, it is important to prioritize them based on importance and feasibility. Importance refers to how meaningful the goal is to us, while feasibility refers to how likely it is that we can achieve the goal given our current resources and circumstances. Prioritizing goals allows us to focus our efforts on what matters most and ensures that we are not overwhelmed or discouraged by setting unrealistic goals.

In conclusion, setting financial goals is an important step in creating a financial plan. By distinguishing between short-term and long-term goals, applying the SMART goal-setting principles, and prioritizing goals based on importance and feasibility, we can stay motivated and focused on achieving financial success.

Here are some examples of financial goals based on different time frames:

Short-term goals (1 year or less):
- Build an emergency fund of $5,000
- Pay off credit card debt of $3,000
- Save up $2,000 for a vacation

Mid-term goals (1-5 years):
- Save $20,000 for a down payment on a house
- Pay off a car loan of $10,000
- Invest $15,000 in a retirement account

Long-term goals (5+ years):

- Save $100,000 for children's college education
- Pay off a mortgage of $200,000
- Build a retirement fund of $500,000

By setting specific, measurable, achievable, relevant, and time-bound (SMART) goals, individuals can better track their progress and work towards achieving their desired outcomes. It's important to prioritize goals based on their importance and feasibility, as this can help individuals stay motivated and focused on what truly matters to them.

IV Benefits of budgeting
Steps to create a budget
Tips for sticking to a budget

A. Benefits of budgeting

Creating and sticking to a budget is an essential part of any financial plan. The benefits of budgeting are numerous and can include:

1. **Increased control over your finances:** Budgeting allows you to track your spending, identify areas where you may be overspending, and make adjustments to stay within your means

2. **Reduced stress:** When you have a clear picture of your financial situation and a plan in place to manage your expenses, you'll likely feel less stressed about money.

3. **Improved financial decision-making:** A budget helps you make informed decisions about where to allocate your money,

whether it's paying off debt, saving for a down payment on a house, or investing for the future.

4. **Increased savings:** When you have a budget in place, you're more likely to save money because you're able to identify areas where you can cut back on expenses.

B. Steps to create a budget

Creating a budget doesn't have to be complicated. Here are some simple steps you can follow:

1. **Determine your monthly income:** Start by calculating your total monthly income, including your salary, any bonuses, and any other sources of income.
2. **List your expenses:** Make a list of all your expenses, including fixed expenses like rent or mortgage payments, utilities, and car payments, as well as variable expenses like groceries, entertainment, and dining out.
3. **Categorize your expenses:** Group your expenses into categories like housing, transportation, food, and entertainment.
4. **Set spending limits:** Once you've categorized your expenses, set spending limits for each category based on your income and financial goals.
5. **Track your spending:** Keep track of your expenses throughout the month to make sure you're staying within your budget.

C. Tips for sticking to a budget

Sticking to a budget can be challenging, but there are some strategies that can help:

1. **Use a budgeting app:** There are many budgeting apps available that can help you track your expenses, set goals, and stay on top of your finances.

2. **Make adjustments as needed**: If you find that you're consistently overspending in a particular category, adjust your budget accordingly.

3. **Automate savings:** Set up automatic transfers from your checking account to a savings account to make saving easier.

4. **Focus on your goals:** Keep your financial goals in mind and remind yourself of them regularly to stay motivated and focused on your budget.

5. **Celebrate your successes:** When you achieve a financial goal or stick to your budget for a certain period of time, celebrate your success to stay motivated and inspired to continue on your financial journey.

V Saving and Investing

- **Different types of savings accounts and investments.**
- **Determining an appropriate savings rate**
- **Assessing risk tolerance and creating an investment portfolio**

Saving and investing are essential components of any financial plan. Saving enables individuals to build a financial cushion that can provide security in times of financial hardship, while investing can help grow wealth over the long term. Here are some important considerations when it comes to saving and investing:

1. **Types of savings accounts and investments:** There are various types of savings accounts and investments available, each with its own benefits and risks. For example, savings accounts offer low risk and easy access to funds, while stocks and mutual funds offer the potential for higher returns but with greater risk. It's important to understand the different options available and choose those that align with your goals and risk tolerance.

2. **Determining an appropriate savings rate:** Once you have identified your financial goals, it's important to determine an appropriate savings rate. This will depend on a variety of factors, such as your income, expenses, and existing debt. Financial experts generally recommend saving at least 20% of your income, but the exact rate will vary depending on individual circumstances.

3. **Assessing risk tolerance and creating an investment portfolio:** Investing can be an effective way to grow wealth over the long term, but it also comes with risk. It's important to assess your risk tolerance and create an investment portfolio that aligns with your goals and level of risk tolerance. A financial advisor can be helpful in this process.

4. **Diversification**: Another important consideration when it comes to investing is diversification. This means spreading your investments across different types of assets, such as stocks, bonds, and real estate, in order to reduce risk. Diversification can help protect your portfolio from the ups and downs of individual assets.

5. **Rebalancing:** It's important to regularly review and rebalance your investment portfolio to ensure it continues to align with your goals and risk tolerance. This may involve selling some

investments and purchasing others in order to maintain the appropriate mix.

Overall, saving and investing are critical components of any financial plan. By understanding the different options available, determining an appropriate savings rate, assessing risk tolerance, and creating a diversified investment portfolio, individuals can build wealth over the long term and achieve their financial goals.

1. **Different types of savings accounts and investments:**

- Savings accounts: These are low-risk options that offer minimal interest rates. They are typically used for emergency funds or short-term savings goals.
- Certificates of Deposit (CDs): CDs are similar to savings accounts but offer higher interest rates in exchange for a fixed-term commitment.
- Stocks: Stocks represent ownership in a company and can offer high returns but also come with higher risk.
- Bonds: Bonds are debt securities issued by companies or governments and offer lower returns but lower risk compared to stocks.

2. **Determining an appropriate savings rate:**
A common rule of thumb is to save at least 15-20% of your income. However, the actual savings rate will depend on your financial goals, current expenses, and income.

3. **Assessing risk tolerance and creating an investment portfolio:**

- Risk tolerance is the level of risk you are comfortable taking on when investing. It is important to determine this before creating an investment portfolio.
- A diversified investment portfolio can help manage risk by spreading investments across different asset classes and industries.
- Examples of asset classes include stocks, bonds, real estate, and commodities.

Overall, saving and investing are important components of a financial plan as they can help grow wealth over time. However, it's important to assess risk tolerance and choose investments based on individual goals and circumstances.

VI Managing Debt
Strategies for paying off debt
Prioritizing debt payments
Consolidation and refinancing options

Strategies for paying off debt

When it comes to paying off debt, there are several strategies that individuals can use to accelerate their progress and achieve financial freedom. Here are a few effective strategies to consider:

The Snowball Method

1. The snowball method involves paying off the smallest debt first, then using the money that would have gone toward that debt to pay off the next smallest debt, and so on. This method is effective because it provides a sense of momentum and progress, which can be motivating. Additionally, as debts

are paid off, there is more money available each month to put towards the remaining debts.

The Avalanche Method

2. The avalanche method involves paying off the debt with the highest interest rate first, then moving on to the debt with the next highest interest rate, and so on. This method can save money on interest charges over time, as the high-interest debt is paid off more quickly.

The Debt Consolidation Loan

3. If an individual has several high-interest debts, consolidating them into a single loan with a lower interest rate can be an effective strategy for paying them off. This can make the debt more manageable, as there is only one monthly payment to make instead of multiple payments.

The Balance Transfer

4. Similar to debt consolidation, a balance transfer involves transferring high-interest debt to a credit card with a lower interest rate. This can save money on interest charges and make it easier to pay off the debt.

No matter which strategy is chosen, it's important to make a plan and stick to it. This may involve cutting back on expenses or finding ways to increase income in order to free up more money to put towards debt payments. Additionally, it's important to avoid taking on new debt while paying off existing debt. With diligence and persistence, it is possible to become debt-free and achieve financial freedom.

Prioritizing debt payments

prioritizing debt payments is an important step in managing debt and becoming financially stable. It involves determining which debts to pay off first based on various factors such as interest rates, balances, and payment terms. Here are some tips for prioritizing debt payments:

1. **List all debts:** Start by listing all debts, including the creditor, interest rate, balance, and minimum monthly payment.
2. **Identify high-interest debts:** Focus on paying off high-interest debts first, as they are the most expensive and can quickly spiral out of control if left unchecked.
3. **Consider payment terms:** Some debts, such as car loans or mortgages, have a fixed payment schedule that cannot be adjusted. Focus on paying off debts that have more flexibility in terms of the payment schedule and interest rates.
4. **Snowball method:** This method involves paying off the smallest debts first while continuing to make minimum payments on larger debts. Once the smallest debt is paid off, move on to the next smallest debt and continue until all debts are paid off.
5. **Avalanche method:** This method involves paying off the debt with the highest interest rate first while continuing to make minimum payments on other debts. Once the highest interest debt is paid off, move on to the next highest interest debt and continue until all debts are paid off.

By prioritizing debt payments, individuals can take control of their finances and work towards becoming debt-free. It requires discipline and commitment, but the benefits of being debt-free are well worth the effort.

Consolidation and refinancing options

Consolidation and refinancing are two strategies that can help individuals manage their debt more effectively.

Debt consolidation involves taking out a single loan to pay off multiple debts, such as credit card balances or personal loans. This can simplify the payment process and potentially lower interest rates, as the new loan may have a lower rate than the previous debts. However, it is important to carefully consider the terms and fees associated with the consolidation loan before proceeding, as some loans may come with hidden costs or longer repayment terms.

Refinancing involves replacing an existing loan or debt with a new one, often with a lower interest rate. This can be beneficial for those with high-interest debts, such as credit card balances or student loans. Refinancing can potentially lower monthly payments and save money on interest over the life of the loan. However, it is important to carefully consider any fees or penalties associated with refinancing and ensure that the new loan has favorable terms.

Overall, consolidation and refinancing can be useful tools for managing debt, but it is important to carefully consider the pros and cons and consult with a financial advisor before proceeding.

Examples of consolidation and refinancing options include

1. Balance transfer credit cards: These cards offer a low or 0% interest rate for a certain period of time (usually 6-18 months) on balances transferred from other credit cards. This can be a good option for high-interest credit card debt.
2. Personal loans: Personal loans can be used to consolidate multiple debts into one loan with a lower interest rate. This can make it easier to manage debt and save money on interest.
3. Home equity loans or lines of credit: These loans allow you to borrow against the equity in your home to pay off high-interest debt. However, this option puts your home at risk if you're unable to make payments.
4. Student loan refinancing: If you have student loans with high-interest rates, you may be able to refinance them for a lower rate. This can help you save money on interest over the life of the loan.
5. Auto loan refinancing: If you have an auto loan with a high-interest rate, you may be able to refinance it for a lower rate. This can help you save money on interest and lower your monthly payments.

VII   Insurance and Estate Planning
Importance of insurance for financial security
Types of insurance to consider
Overview of estate planning and creating a will

Insurance is an important component of a comprehensive financial plan as it provides protection against unforeseen circumstances that can cause financial hardship. Having adequate insurance coverage can provide peace of mind and help individuals and families manage unexpected events such as accidents, illness, disability, or death.

For example, health insurance can help cover the cost of medical treatment, including surgeries, hospital stays, and prescription medications. Disability insurance can provide income replacement in case an individual is unable to work due to injury or illness. Homeowner's insurance can protect against damage to property caused by natural disasters, theft, or other unforeseen events. Life insurance can provide financial support to loved ones in case of the policyholder's death.

Having insurance coverage can also help protect one's financial assets and investments. Without adequate insurance coverage, individuals may be forced to dip into their savings or liquidate their assets to cover the cost of unexpected events. This can have a significant impact on their financial well-being and future plans.

Overall, it is important to assess one's insurance needs based on individual circumstances and risk tolerance. This can involve considering factors such as age, health status, family size, income, and overall financial goals. By obtaining the appropriate insurance coverage, individuals can help secure their financial future and protect themselves and their loved ones against unexpected events.

Here are several types of insurance that individuals should consider when creating a financial plan.

Some of the most common types of insurance include:

1. Health insurance: This type of insurance is essential for covering medical expenses in the event of an illness or injury. Health insurance can include coverage for doctor visits, hospital stays, prescription drugs, and other medical expenses.

2. Life insurance: Life insurance provides financial protection for your loved ones in the event of your unexpected death. It can help cover expenses such as funeral costs, outstanding debts, and provide income replacement for your dependents.

3. Disability insurance: Disability insurance provides income replacement if you become unable to work due to an injury or illness. This type of insurance can help cover living expenses and other financial obligations during a period of disability.

4. Auto insurance: Auto insurance is mandatory in most states and provides coverage in the event of an accident or theft. It can help cover the cost of repairs or replacement of your vehicle, as well as any liability you may have for damages to others.

5. Homeowner's or renter's insurance: This type of insurance provides coverage for your home or rental property and its contents in the event of damage or loss due to fire, theft, or other covered events.

It is important to carefully consider your individual needs and risks when deciding which types of insurance to purchase. Working with a financial advisor can help you determine the appropriate types and amounts of insurance for your situation.

Overview of estate planning and creating a will

Estate planning involves making decisions about how you want your assets to be distributed after your death, and whom you want to manage your affairs if you become incapacitated. It's an important part of financial planning that can help ensure that your wishes are carried out and that your loved ones are taken care of.

One of the key components of estate planning is creating a will. A will is a legal document that outlines how you want your assets to be distributed after your death. It allows you to name an executor, who will be responsible for managing your estate and can also name guardians for your minor children.

Other important documents to consider as part of your estate plan include a living will, which outlines your wishes for medical treatment if you become incapacitated, and a power of attorney, which allows someone you trust to make financial or legal decisions on your behalf if you are unable to do so.

It's important to regularly review and update your estate plan as your circumstances change. This can include changes in your family situation, such as births, deaths, or marriages, as well as changes in your financial situation, such as significant changes in your assets or debts.

By taking the time to create an estate plan, you can help ensure that your wishes are carried out and that your loved ones are taken care of in the event of your death or incapacitation.

Here are the steps to estate planning and creating a will:

1. Take inventory of your assets and debts: The first step is to create a list of all your assets and debts, including bank accounts, investments, real estate, and personal property. This will help you determine the value of your estate and identify any potential issues that may need to be addressed.

2. Choose an executor: An executor is responsible for managing your estate after you pass away. You should choose someone who is trustworthy and capable of handling the responsibilities.

3. Consider guardianship: If you have minor children, you should name a guardian to care for them if you pass away.

4. Create a will: A will is a legal document that outlines your wishes for how your assets will be distributed after you pass away. You can include instructions for who will receive your property, how your debts will be paid, and who will be responsible for managing your estate.

5. Consider a trust: A trust is a legal arrangement in which a trustee holds and manages assets for the benefit of a beneficiary. It can be used to manage your assets during your lifetime and after your death.

6. Review and update your plan regularly: It's important to review and update your estate plan regularly to ensure that it reflects your current wishes and circumstances.

7. Consider working with an estate planning attorney: An estate planning attorney can provide guidance and assistance in creating an estate plan that meets your specific needs and goals.

In conclusion, estate planning and creating a will are critical components of a comprehensive financial plan. By taking the time to assess one's current financial situation, set financial goals, create a budget, save and invest wisely, manage debt, and obtain appropriate insurance coverage, individuals can achieve financial security for themselves and their loved ones. The final step of estate planning, including creating a will and making provisions for one's assets after death, ensures that their wishes are respected and their loved ones are taken care of. With the right mindset, education, and guidance, anyone can create a solid financial plan and secure their financial future.

VIII. Monitoring and Adjusting Your Plan

- **Regularly reviewing and updating your financial plan**
- **Identifying changes in circumstances that may require adjustments**
- **Celebrating successes and reassessing goals**

I. Monitoring and Adjusting Your Plan

Creating a financial plan is not a one-time event. Your financial situation and goals may change over time, and it is important to regularly review and adjust your plan accordingly. Monitoring and adjusting your plan can help ensure that you stay on track and achieve your financial goals.

One important aspect of monitoring your plan is reviewing your budget and expenses regularly. This can help you identify areas where you may be overspending or where you can cut back. It can also help you track your progress towards your savings goals and make adjustments as needed.

Another important aspect of monitoring your plan is reviewing your investment portfolio. As your financial situation and goals change, you may need to adjust the risk level of your investments or rebalance your portfolio to ensure that it aligns with your goals.

In addition to monitoring your plan, it is important to be flexible and willing to make changes when necessary. Life is unpredictable, and unexpected events such as job loss or illness can impact your financial situation. Being open to adjusting your plan can help you adapt to these changes and stay on track towards your goals.

Overall, monitoring and adjusting your financial plan is an ongoing process. By regularly reviewing your budget, investments, and goals, and being flexible and willing to make changes when necessary, you can ensure that your plan remains relevant and effective in helping you achieve financial success.

Here are some examples of monitoring and adjusting your financial plan:

1. **Review your budget** on a monthly basis to see if you are on track to meet your financial goals. If you notice that you are overspending in certain categories, you may need to adjust your budget accordingly.

2. **Checking your investment portfolio** quarterly or annually to make sure that your investments are performing well and are aligned with your risk tolerance and financial goals. If you notice that certain investments are underperforming, you may need to re-evaluate your portfolio and make changes as necessary.

3. **Assessing your debt repayment plan** regularly to see if you are making progress towards paying off your debts. If you are not making enough progress, you may need to restructure your debt payments or seek professional help.

4. **Re-evaluate your insurance coverage** annually to make sure that you have adequate coverage for your changing needs. For example, if you have recently started a family, you may need to increase your life insurance coverage.

5. **Updating your estate plan as your life circumstances change**, such as getting married or divorced, having children, or acquiring new assets. This can help ensure that your assets are distributed according to your wishes and that your loved ones are provided for in the event of your death.

By regularly monitoring and adjusting your financial plan, you can stay on track towards achieving your financial goals and adapt to any changes or challenges that may arise along the way.

Identifying changes in circumstances that may require adjustments to your financial plan is an important step in ensuring its continued success. Life is unpredictable and events such as job loss, marriage, divorce, the birth of a child, or a sudden illness can significantly impact your financial situation.

When such changes occur, it is important to reassess your financial plan and make the necessary adjustments. For example, if you experience a job loss or reduction in income, you may need to reduce your expenses and adjust your savings and investment goals. On the other hand, if you receive a significant inheritance, you may need to consider how to best invest or allocate those funds in line with your financial goals.

Other changes that may require adjustments to your financial plan include changes in tax laws, changes in your risk tolerance, or changes in your long-term financial goals. Regularly reviewing and monitoring your financial plan can help you stay on track towards achieving your goals and make any necessary adjustments along the way.

It is important to remember that a financial plan is not a one-time exercise, but rather an ongoing process. As your life and the financial situation evolves, your financial plan should also evolve to ensure that it continues to align with your goals and values. Regularly reviewing and updating your plan can help ensure that you are well-positioned to achieve financial success and security in the long term.

Celebrating successes and reassessing goals

Creating a financial plan can be a daunting task, but it's an essential step towards achieving financial freedom. As we work towards our goals, it's important to celebrate our successes and reassess our goals periodically to ensure we stay on track.

Celebrating successes is crucial to maintain motivation and momentum towards our financial goals. When we achieve a milestone, it's important to take time to reflect on our progress and acknowledge the hard work that went into reaching that point. Celebrating successes can also help us maintain a positive attitude towards our financial journey, which can make it more enjoyable and less stressful.

However, it's equally important to reassess our goals periodically to ensure they are still relevant and achievable. Our financial circumstances can change over time, and what may have been a priority a year ago may not be as important now. By reassessing our goals, we can make sure we are still working towards the things that matter most to us and adjust our plan accordingly.

When reassessing our goals, it's important to consider both short-term and long-term goals.

Short-term goals may include paying off debt, building an emergency fund, or saving for a vacation. Long-term goals may include saving for retirement, buying a home, or starting a business. It's important to ensure that our goals are specific, measurable, achievable, relevant, and time-bound (SMART), so we can track our progress and make adjustments as needed.

Another important aspect of reassessing our goals is to take stock of our current financial situation.

Are we making progress towards our goals, or are we falling behind? Are there any unexpected expenses or changes in income that may impact our ability to achieve our goals? By taking a closer look at our finances, we can identify any areas that may need improvement and make necessary adjustments to our plan.

In conclusion, celebrating successes and reassessing our goals are both critical components of creating a successful financial plan. By taking time to acknowledge our progress and adjust our plan as needed, we can stay on track towards achieving our financial goals and ultimately achieve financial freedom.

IX. Resources and Tools

- **Online resources and tools for financial planning**
- **Financial advisors and when to seek professional help**
- **Recommendations for further reading and education**

Online resources and tools for financial planning

in today's digital age, there are numerous online resources and tools available to assist individuals in creating and managing their financial plans. These resources can help simplify the process, provide guidance, and offer valuable insights. In this section, we will explore some of the most popular online resources and tools for financial planning.

Personal Finance Websites

1. There are several personal finance websites available that offer a wealth of information on budgeting, saving, investing, and more. Some popular examples include:
   - Mint: This free online budgeting tool allows you to track your spending, set financial goals, and monitor your credit score.
   - NerdWallet: This website provides personalized advice on credit cards, mortgages, insurance, and other financial products.
   - Investopedia: This site offers a wide range of educational resources on investing, personal finance, and market news.

Robo-Advisors

2. Robo-advisors are automated investment platforms that use algorithms to provide customized investment portfolios based on an individual's goals and risk tolerance. Some popular robo-advisors include:

- Betterment: This platform offers a range of investment portfolios tailored to your goals and risk tolerance, and charges low fees.
- Wealthfront: This robo-advisor offers a variety of investment options, including retirement accounts and college savings plans.

Budgeting and Saving Apps

3. There are numerous mobile apps available that can help you track your spending, set savings goals, and even invest your money. Some popular examples include:

- Acorns: This app rounds up your purchases and invests the spare change in a diversified portfolio.
- YNAB (You Need a Budget): This budgeting app helps you track your spending, create a budget, and save money for specific goals.

Retirement Planning Tools

4. There are several online tools available to help you plan for retirement, including:

- AARP Retirement Calculator: This tool helps you estimate how much you need to save for retirement based on your age, income, and other factors.

- Social Security Administration Retirement Estimator: This calculator provides an estimate of your Social Security benefits based on your earnings history.

Tax Preparation Software

5. Tax preparation can be a daunting task, but there are several online tools available to help simplify the process. Some popular tax preparation software includes:
   - TurboTax: This software offers step-by-step guidance for preparing your tax return and can even file your taxes electronically.
   - H&R Block: This software provides tax preparation services and also offers online tax filing.

   In conclusion, there are a wide variety of online resources and tools available to assist individuals in creating and managing their financial plans. Whether you're looking for budgeting advice, investment guidance, or retirement planning tools, there's sure to be an online resource or tool that meets your needs. It's important to do your research and choose reputable sources that align with your goals and values.

Financial advisors and when to seek professional help

Financial planning can be a complex and challenging process, and it can be beneficial to seek the advice of a financial advisor to help navigate the various decisions and strategies involved in building a solid financial plan. While some people may be able to successfully manage their finances on their own, others may benefit from the expertise and guidance of a professional.

There are many different types of financial advisors, each with their own areas of expertise and ways of working with clients. Some advisors may specialize in retirement planning, while others may focus on investment strategies or debt management. When choosing a financial advisor, it's important to consider their qualifications, experience, and fee structure, as well as whether their approach and values align with your own.

So when should you seek the help of a financial advisor? Here are some situations where it may be beneficial to work with a professional:

1. You're going through a major life transition. Whether it's getting married, starting a family, buying a home, or going through a divorce, major life events can have significant financial implications. A financial advisor can help you navigate these transitions and make informed decisions that align with your long-term goals.

2. You're feeling overwhelmed or uncertain about your finances. If you're struggling to make sense of your financial situation or feeling unsure about how to move forward, a financial advisor can provide clarity and guidance.

3. You're approaching retirement. As you are near retirement age, it's important to have a solid plan in place to ensure that you can comfortably meet your financial needs in retirement. A financial advisor can help you evaluate your options and create a strategy that aligns with your goals.

4. You're looking to maximize your investments. If you're interested in investing but unsure where to start or how to optimize your portfolio, a financial advisor can help you

develop a comprehensive investment strategy that takes your risk tolerance, goals, and timeline into account.

5. You're looking to improve your overall financial health. A financial advisor can help you evaluate your current financial situation and develop a plan to improve your financial health, whether that involves paying down debt, saving for the future, or increasing your income.

While working with a financial advisor can be beneficial, it's important to note that not all advisors are created equal. Before choosing an advisor, be sure to do your research, ask for references, and consider their track record and experience. You should also be clear on their fee structure and make sure it aligns with your budget and goals.

In summary, while it's possible to manage your finances on your own, working with a financial advisor can provide valuable guidance and support, particularly in complex situations or during major life transitions. When choosing an advisor, be sure to consider their qualifications, experience, and fee structure, and make sure that their approach and values align with your own.

Recommendations for further reading and education

Recommendations for further reading and education are critical for individuals who want to improve their financial literacy and develop a comprehensive financial plan. Learning about personal finance can be overwhelming, but there are numerous resources available to help individuals navigate the process.

1. There are countless books available on personal finance, from beginner level to advanced. Some popular titles include "The Total Money Makeover" by Dave Ramsey, "The Millionaire Next Door" by Thomas J. Stanley and William D. Danko, "Rich Dad Poor Dad" by Robert Kiyosaki, and "The Intelligent Investor" by Benjamin Graham

2. Online courses offer a convenient way to learn about personal finance at your own pace. Some popular platforms for online courses include Coursera, Udemy, and edX. There are also many free courses available through websites like Khan Academy and Investopedia.

3. Podcasts have become increasingly popular in recent years, and there are numerous options available for those interested in personal finance. Some popular podcasts include "The Dave Ramsey Show," "Afford Anything" with Paula Pant, and "The Clark Howard Show."

4. Financial advisors can provide professional guidance and help develop a comprehensive financial plan. They can also provide ongoing support and monitor progress towards financial goals. However, it is important to carefully research and select a reputable and qualified financial advisor.

5. Social media platforms like Twitter, Instagram, and LinkedIn can provide valuable insights and tips on personal finance. Online communities such as Reddit's "Personal Finance" and "Financial Independence" subreddits can also offer support and advice from a community of individuals with similar goals.

In conclusion, there are numerous resources available to individuals who want to improve their financial literacy and develop a comprehensive financial plan. It is essential to take advantage of these resources and continue to learn and grow financially.

CHAPTER - 4

BUDGETING: TIPS AND STRATEGIES FOR CREATING AND STICKING TO A BUDGET

Introduction

Budgeting is a crucial aspect of personal finance that can help individuals achieve financial security and success. By definition, a budget is a financial plan that outlines an individual's income and expenses, along with their financial goals, and helps them allocate their resources effectively. In essence, a budget is a roadmap to financial stability, providing individuals with the necessary tools to manage their money and make informed financial decisions.

Budgeting is important for several reasons. First, it helps individuals understand their financial situation by providing a clear picture of their income and expenses. By creating a budget, individuals can identify areas where they may be overspending or underspending and make necessary adjustments to achieve their financial goals.

Second, budgeting helps individuals avoid debt and financial troubles. By tracking their expenses and income, individuals can avoid overspending and ensure that they have enough money to cover their expenses. This can help prevent individuals from falling into debt, which can have long-term negative consequences on their financial health.

Third, budgeting can help individuals achieve their financial goals, such as saving for a down payment on a home, paying off debt, or building an emergency fund. By setting financial goals and allocating funds to specific categories, individuals can prioritize their spending and work towards achieving their objectives.

Creating a budget involves several steps. The first step is to identify one's income and expenses. This includes all sources of income, such as salaries, bonuses, and investment income, as well as all expenses, such as rent, utilities, food, and transportation. It is important to be as comprehensive as possible when identifying expenses to ensure that nothing is overlooked.

The next step is to categorize expenses into fixed and variable expenses. Fixed expenses are those that remain the same each month, such as rent or mortgage payments, while variable expenses change from month to month, such as groceries or entertainment expenses.

Once expenses are categorized, it is important to set financial goals and allocate funds to specific categories. This involves prioritizing spending and determining how much money should be allocated to each category. This can be done using budgeting tools and software, which can help individuals track their spending and adjust their budget as necessary.

Sticking to a budget can be challenging, but there are several tips and strategies that can help. These include making budgeting a habit, tracking expenses regularly, finding ways to reduce expenses, and dealing with unexpected expenses. It is also important to monitor and adjust the budget regularly to ensure that it remains aligned with one's financial goals.

Budgeting is not a one-size-fits-all approach and may need to be adjusted for different life stages. For example, college students may have different budgeting considerations than those starting a family or planning for retirement. Adjusting the budget to accommodate changing circumstances is key to achieving financial success.

Budgeting can also impact relationships, particularly in a shared household. Communication about money and budgeting is important to ensure that everyone is on the same page and working towards common financial goals.

In conclusion, budgeting is an essential component of personal finance that can help individuals achieve financial security and success. By creating a budget, individuals can gain a clear understanding of their financial situation, avoid debt and financial troubles, and work towards achieving their financial goals. It is important to make budgeting a habit, monitor expenses regularly, adjust the budget as necessary, and communicate about money and budgeting with others.

II Benefits of Budgeting

Budgeting is a fundamental tool that can help individuals to manage their finances effectively. It allows people to plan their spending, manage their debt, and achieve their financial goals. In this section, we will discuss the benefits of budgeting and how it can help individuals achieve their financial goals while avoiding debt and financial troubles.

One of the most significant benefits of budgeting is that it helps individuals achieve their financial goals. Budgeting allows people to prioritize their spending and allocate their money towards the things that matter most to them. For example, individuals can allocate funds towards saving for a down payment on a house, paying off student loans, or investing in retirement accounts. By having a clear plan for their finances, individuals are more likely to achieve their financial goals and realize their long-term financial aspirations.

Another benefit of budgeting is that it helps individuals avoid debt and financial troubles. Without a budget, it can be easy to overspend and accumulate debt. However, by having a clear plan for their finances, individuals can avoid overspending and ensure that they have enough money to cover their expenses. Additionally, budgeting can help individuals identify areas where they can cut back on spending, such as eating out less or reducing entertainment expenses. By reducing their expenses, individuals can save more money, pay off their debts faster, and avoid financial troubles.

Furthermore, budgeting can help individuals to develop good financial habits. By regularly tracking their expenses and reviewing their budget, individuals can become more mindful of their spending and make more informed financial decisions. Additionally, budgeting can help individuals to prioritize their spending, avoid impulse purchases, and become more disciplined with their finances. These habits can have long-term benefits and help individuals to achieve financial security and success.

In conclusion, budgeting is an essential tool that can help individuals achieve their financial goals and avoid debt and financial troubles. By prioritizing spending, developing good financial habits, and becoming more mindful of their expenses, individuals can become more disciplined with their finances and achieve financial security and success. The next section will discuss how to create a budget and the steps involved.

Creating a Budget

Creating a budget is a crucial step in achieving financial stability and success. It allows individuals to understand their financial situation, set realistic goals, and make informed decisions about their spending and saving habits. Here are some steps to follow when creating a budget:

Identifying income and expenses: The first step in creating a budget is to determine your sources of income and expenses. This involves collecting and reviewing financial statements, bills, and receipts to get an accurate understanding of your cash flow.

Categorizing expenses: Once you have identified all your expenses, the next step is to categorize them. This allows you to see where your money is going and helps you identify areas where you can cut back or reduce spending.

Setting financial goals: It's important to have specific financial goals in mind when creating a budget. This gives you something to work towards and helps you stay motivated. Goals can include saving for a down payment on a house, paying off debt, or saving for retirement.

Allocating funds to categories: Once you have categorized your expenses and identified your financial goals, you can allocate funds to each category. This involves setting a budget for each category and sticking to it.

Using budgeting tools and software: There are many tools and software available to help with budgeting, such as spreadsheets, apps, and online tools. These can help automate the process and make it easier to track your spending and progress towards your financial goals.

IV Tips for Sticking to a Budget

Creating a budget is one thing, but sticking to it can be a challenge for many individuals. However, it is important to follow a budget in order to achieve financial goals and avoid debt. Here are some tips for sticking to a budget:

1. Make budgeting a habit: It takes time and effort to make budgeting a habit, but it is important to do so in order to successfully stick to a budget. Set aside a specific time each week to review and adjust the budget if necessary, and track all expenses in a designated place.

2. Strategies for tracking expenses: There are many ways to track expenses, such as using an app, spreadsheet, or even pen and paper. Find a method that works best for you and make sure to record all expenses, even small ones, to get an accurate picture of where your money is going.

3. Ways to reduce expenses: To stick to a budget, it is important to find ways to reduce expenses. This can include cutting back on unnecessary expenses such as dining out or entertainment, finding ways to save on utilities and other bills, and using coupons or shopping for deals.

4. Techniques for dealing with unexpected expenses: Unexpected expenses, such as a car repair or medical bill, can throw off a budget. To deal with these expenses, it is important to have an emergency fund set aside to cover unexpected costs. If an emergency fund is not available, consider temporarily adjusting the budget to accommodate the unexpected expense.

5. The importance of monitoring and adjusting the budget: A budget should not be set in stone. It is important to monitor

the budget regularly and make adjustments as necessary. Life circumstances and expenses can change, so it is important to make sure the budget reflects those changes.

By following these tips, individuals can successfully stick to their budget and achieve their financial goals.

V Dealing with Budgeting Challenges

Creating and sticking to a budget can be challenging at times, but it is an essential step towards financial security and stability. In this section, we will discuss some common challenges that people face while budgeting and strategies to overcome them.

Common challenges to budgeting:

a. Unexpected expenses: Unexpected expenses such as medical emergencies, car repairs, or home maintenance can quickly derail a budget.

b. Overspending: Overspending on non-essential items can lead to a budget deficit, making it harder to achieve financial goals.

c. Lack of discipline: It can be challenging to stick to a budget without discipline and self-control.

d. Lack of motivation: Staying motivated to stick to a budget can be difficult, especially if financial goals seem distant or unattainable.

Strategies for overcoming these challenges:

a. Emergency fund: Creating an emergency fund can help mitigate the impact of unexpected expenses on a budget. Aim to have at least three to six months of living expenses in savings.

b. Prioritizing expenses: Prioritizing essential expenses such as rent, utilities, and groceries can help to ensure that these expenses are covered before allocating funds to discretionary spending.

c. Setting limits: Setting limits on discretionary spending and developing a plan for how to spend within those limits can help to avoid overspending.

d. Automating savings: Setting up automatic transfers to a savings account or investment account can help to stay disciplined and make saving a habit.

e. Using budgeting apps and tools: There are various budgeting apps and tools available that can help track spending, set savings goals, and monitor progress.

How to deal with setbacks and stay motivated:

a. **Reevaluate financial goals**: If setbacks occur, reevaluating financial goals and adjusting the budget accordingly can help to get back on track.

b. **Celebrate small victories:** Celebrating small victories such as paying off a debt or staying within a budget for a month can help to stay motivated and make progress towards financial goals.

c **Seek support:** Seeking support from friends, family, or a financial advisor can provide encouragement and accountability.

In conclusion, while budgeting can present challenges, it is essential to achieving financial security and stability. Developing strategies to overcome these challenges and staying motivated to stick to a budget can lead to long-term financial success.

VI Budgeting for Different Life Stages

Budgeting is not a one-size-fits-all solution, and different life stages can come with unique financial challenges and priorities. In this section, we will explore some of the budgeting considerations for various life stages.

1. Budgeting for College

For college students, managing money is often a new experience. While some may have had part-time jobs during high school, college can be the first time they are fully responsible for their finances. Here are some tips for budgeting during college:

- Calculate your income: Determine your income sources, such as part-time jobs, scholarships, or financial aid.
- Track your expenses: Keep track of your expenses, such as tuition fees, textbooks, food, transportation, and entertainment.
- Create a realistic budget: Based on your income and expenses, create a realistic budget that you can stick to.
- Look for ways to save: Find ways to save on expenses, such as buying used textbooks, cooking meals at home, or using student discounts.

2. Budgeting for Starting a Family

is an exciting time, but it can also come with added financial responsibilities. Here are some tips for budgeting during this stage:

- Review your expenses: Take a look at your current expenses and determine what expenses may increase with the addition of a child.

- Plan for childcare costs: Childcare costs can be a significant expense, so plan ahead and research options that fit your budget.
- Set up an emergency fund: Unexpected expenses can arise when starting a family, so it's important to have an emergency fund in place.
- Adjust your budget as needed: As your family grows and changes, adjust your budget to accommodate for new expenses or changes in income.

3. Budgeting for Retirement

Retirement is a time when you may no longer have a steady income from work, so it's important to budget carefully to ensure you have enough savings to support your lifestyle. Here are some tips for budgeting during retirement:

- Determine your retirement income: Calculate your retirement income sources, such as social security, pension, or retirement savings.
- Estimate your retirement expenses: Estimate your retirement expenses, such as housing, healthcare, and leisure activities.
- Create a retirement budget: Based on your income and expenses, create a budget that ensures you can cover your expenses without depleting your savings too quickly.
- Consider downsizing: If your current living expenses are too high, consider downsizing to a smaller home to reduce expenses.
- Monitor your budget: Continuously monitor your budget to ensure you're on track to meet your retirement goals

Overall, budgeting for different life stages involves identifying your financial priorities, estimating your income and expenses, and creating a realistic budget that you can stick to. It's important to regularly review and adjust your budget as your life circumstances change.

VII Budgeting and Relationships

When it comes to budgeting, it is important to recognize that it is not just an individual effort but can also involve those closest to us, such as our partners or family members. In this section, we will discuss how to budget as a couple or in a shared household, as well as tips for communicating about money and budgeting with others.

How to budget as a couple or in a shared household

1. When budgeting as a couple or in a shared household, it is important to have open and honest communication about financial goals and priorities. This can involve discussing income, expenses, debts, and savings. It may also be helpful to designate one person as the primary budgeter or to split the responsibilities equally. Additionally, it may be necessary to establish guidelines or rules for spending, such as setting a limit on discretionary expenses or agreeing to consult each other before making large purchases.

Tips for communicating about money and budgeting with a partner or family member

2. Effective communication is key to successful budgeting in relationships. Some tips for communicating about money and budgeting with a partner or family member include:

- Be honest and transparent about your financial situation
- Listen actively to the other person's concerns and goals
- Avoid blame or judgment when discussing finances
- Set aside regular times to discuss finances and budgeting
- Celebrate successes and reassess goals together

It is also important to remember that everyone has different attitudes and beliefs about money, which can influence their spending habits and financial priorities. Being aware of these differences and finding ways to compromise can help ensure a successful budgeting partnership.

Overall, budgeting can be a collaborative effort that strengthens relationships and builds financial security. By communicating effectively and working together, couples and families can achieve their financial goals and thrive financially.

In conclusion, budgeting is an essential tool for achieving financial success and security. By creating a budget, individuals can identify their income, expenses, and financial goals and allocate funds accordingly. The benefits of budgeting include better money management, increased savings, reduced debt, and improved financial health.

However, sticking to a budget can be challenging, and individuals may face setbacks and unexpected expenses. Strategies for overcoming budgeting challenges include making budgeting a habit, tracking expenses, reducing expenses, and adjusting the budget as necessary. Additionally, budgeting considerations will vary depending on an individual's life stage, such as college, starting a family, or retirement.

Budgeting can also be a collaborative effort, particularly for couples or those living in shared households. Communication is key when it comes to budgeting and discussing financial goals and strategies with a partner or family member can help ensure everyone is on the same page.

Overall, budgeting requires dedication and effort, but the rewards can be significant. By creating and sticking to a budget, individuals can take control of their finances and work towards achieving their financial goals. Remember to monitor and adjust the budget as needed, and don't be discouraged by setbacks. With a little discipline and perseverance, anyone can achieve financial success through budgeting.

CHAPTER 5

INVESTING BASICS: AN OVERVIEW OF INVESTING AND HOW TO GET STARTED

I Introduction

Investing is an essential part of achieving long-term financial growth and security. It provides the opportunity to grow your wealth and make your money work for you. However, many people are intimidated by investing and don't know where to start.

In this chapter, we will provide an overview of what investing is and how it works, as well as why it is important for financial growth and security. We will also outline the key points of the chapter with examples to help you understand the basics of investing and how to get started.

Investing involves putting your money into assets that have the potential to increase in value over time. These assets can include stocks, bonds, mutual funds, real estate, and more. By investing your money, you are essentially allowing it to grow through the power of compound interest.

The benefits of investing are numerous. It can help you achieve your financial goals, such as saving for retirement, buying a home, or paying for your children's education. Investing can also help you beat inflation, which is the rate at which the cost of goods and services increases over time. Inflation erodes the purchasing power of your money, so investing is a way to protect against this.

The thesis statement of this chapter is that by understanding the basics of investing, you can start to make informed decisions about your money and take advantage of the opportunities that investing offers. We will discuss the different types of investments, the risks and rewards of investing, and how to get started with investing. With this knowledge, you will be able to create a sound investment plan that can help you achieve your financial goals and secure your financial future.

II Benefits of Investing

Investing is one of the most effective ways to grow wealth over time and achieve financial goals. In this chapter, we will explore the benefits of investing and how it can help individuals build long-term wealth, earn passive income, and beat inflation.

One of the most significant benefits of investing is the potential to generate wealth. Unlike traditional savings accounts or certificates of deposit (CDs), investing offers the possibility of higher returns on your money. By investing in stocks, bonds, or mutual funds, you can earn a return on your investment that is typically higher than the interest rate on savings accounts or CDs.

Another advantage of investing is the opportunity to earn passive income. This can come in the form of dividends from stocks or interest payments from bonds. With passive income, your money works for you even when you're not actively managing your investments, allowing you to build wealth without having to put in the extra effort.

Investing can also help individuals beat inflation, which is the rate at which prices increase over time. Inflation can erode the purchasing power of your money, making it less valuable in the future. By investing in assets that appreciate in value over time, such as stocks or real estate, you can potentially earn returns that outpace inflation.

Compared to other forms of saving, such as savings accounts or CDs, investing has the potential to offer much higher returns. While savings accounts and CDs may offer a guaranteed rate of return, the rates are typically low and may not even keep up with inflation. Investing in the stock market, on the other hand, has historically provided average returns of around 10% per year.

Real-life examples of successful investors can demonstrate the benefits of investing. For instance, Warren Buffett, one of the most successful investors of all time, has built his fortune by investing in the stock market over several decades. His investment strategy involves identifying undervalued companies with strong fundamentals and holding onto them for the long term. Another example is Ray Dalio, the founder of Bridgewater Associates, who has generated impressive returns for his clients by investing in a diverse range of assets and using data-driven analysis to inform his investment decisions.

In summary, investing offers a range of benefits, including the potential to generate wealth, earn passive income, and beat inflation. Compared to traditional savings accounts and CDs, investing can provide much higher returns over the long term. Real-life examples of successful investors can serve as inspiration for individuals looking to start investing and build their wealth over time.

Here are some examples of successful investors and their returns:

1. Warren Buffett - Over the past 55 years, Buffett's investment company, Berkshire Hathaway, has delivered an average annual

return of 20.8%. For comparison, the S&P 500 has returned an average of 9.8% over the same period.

2. Peter Lynch - As the manager of Fidelity's Magellan Fund from 1977 to 1990, Lynch delivered an average annual return of 29.2%. During his tenure, the fund outperformed the S&P 500 by an average of 13.4 percentage points per year.

3. Ray Dalio - As the founder of Bridgewater Associates, Dalio has built a reputation as a top-performing hedge fund manager. His flagship fund, Pure Alpha, has delivered an average annual return of 11.5% since its inception in 1991.

4. John Paulson - In 2007, Paulson made a massive bet against the subprime mortgage market, earning a return of more than 500% for his hedge fund. In total, Paulson's funds have delivered an average annual return of 16.7% since 1994.

It's important to note that these examples are not indicative of typical investment returns, and past performance is not a guarantee of future results. However, they do illustrate the potential for significant wealth creation through investing.

III Types of Investments

Investing can take many different forms, with each type of investment carrying its own unique benefits, risks, and potential returns. Below are some of the most common types of investments available to individuals.

1. Stocks: Stocks represent a share of ownership in a company, and can be bought and sold on stock exchanges. Investing in stocks can offer the potential for high returns, but also comes with a high level of risk. It's important to research individual companies and diversify your portfolio to minimize risk.

2. Bonds: Bonds are essentially loans made to companies or governments, with the investor receiving regular interest payments and the return of their principal investment upon maturity. Bonds are generally considered lower risk than stocks but also offer lower potential returns.

3. Mutual Funds: A mutual fund is a collection of stocks, bonds, or other investments that are managed by a professional fund manager. Investing in a mutual fund can offer diversification and professional management, but also comes with fees and the potential for lower returns.

4. Exchange-Traded Funds (ETFs): ETFs are similar to mutual funds in that they are a collection of stocks, bonds, or other investments. However, they are traded on stock exchanges like individual stocks and often have lower fees than mutual funds.

5. Real Estate: Investing in real estate can take many forms, from buying and renting out a property to investing in a Real Estate Investment Trust (REIT). Real estate can offer the potential for high returns, but also comes with a high level of risk and requires significant upfront capital.

6. Commodities: Commodities are raw materials or resources such as gold, oil, or agricultural products. Investing in commodities can offer diversification and a hedge against inflation, but also comes with high volatility and potential for losses.

7. Cryptocurrency: Cryptocurrencies such as Bitcoin or Ethereum are digital assets that can be bought and sold like stocks or other investments. Cryptocurrency can offer the potential for high returns but also comes with high volatility and regulatory uncertainty.

It's important to remember that every investment carries risk, and it's crucial to do your own research and consult with a financial advisor before making any investment decisions. Diversifying your portfolio across different types of investments can help manage risk and potentially increase returns over time.

Investment Type	Potential Rewards	Potential Risks
Stocks	High returns, potential for long-term growth	High volatility, risk of losing principal
Bonds	Fixed income, relatively low-risk	Low returns compared to other types of investments
Mutual Funds	Diversification, professional management	Fees, potential for underperformance
Real Estate	Potential for rental income, property appreciation	Property maintenance, market fluctuations
Commodities	Potential for price appreciation	High volatility, risk of loss
Options	High potential returns	High risk, complex investment strategy
Crypto currencies	High potential returns	High volatility, lack of regulation and security

It's important to note that these are just generalizations, and the actual risks and rewards of any investment can vary greatly based on factors such as the specific investment vehicle, market conditions, and individual circumstances. It's always important to do your own research and consult with a financial professional before making any investment decisions.

Type of Investment	Risk Level	Potential Returns	Liquidity	Investment Period	Examples
Stocks	High	High	High	Long-term	Apple, Amazon, Microsoft
Bonds	Low to Medium	Low to Medium	High	Short to Long-term	US Treasury Bonds, Corporate Bonds
Mutual Funds	Low to Medium	Low to High	Medium to High	Short to Long-term	Vanguard 500 Index Fund, Fidelity Total Bond Fund
ETFs	Low to Medium	Low to High	Medium to High	Short to Long-term	SPDR S&P 500 ETF, iShares Core MSCI EAFE ETF
Real Estate	High	High	Low	Long-term	Rental properties, REITs
Commodities	High	High	Low	Short to Long-term	Gold, Silver, Oil
Crypto currencies	High	High	Low	Short to Long-term	Bitcoin, Ethereum, Litecoin

This table can give a quick overview of the different types of investments, their risk levels, potential returns, liquidity, investment periods, and examples. However, it's important to note that this is not an exhaustive list of investments and that each individual investment within a category may have its own unique characteristics and risks.

IV Investment Strategies

Investing is not just about choosing the right investments, but also about implementing effective investment strategies. There are various investment strategies that investors can use to help them achieve their investment goals. In this section, we will discuss some of the most popular investment strategies, their pros and cons, and how to implement them in practice.

Dollar-Cost Averaging

Dollar-cost averaging (DCA) is an investment strategy that involves investing a fixed amount of money into an investment at regular intervals, regardless of its price. This means that when the price of the investment is low, the investor will buy more shares, and when the price is high, the investor will buy fewer shares. By investing a fixed amount of money at regular intervals, the investor can reduce the impact of market fluctuations on their portfolio.

Pros:

- Reduces the risk of investing a large sum of money at the wrong time

- Takes emotions out of investing, as the investor is not trying to time the market
- Can lead to lower average purchase prices over time

Cons:

- May not maximize returns in a rapidly rising market
- Requires discipline to stick to the investment plan, even during market downturns
- Can result in missed opportunities if the investor is not fully invested during a market rally

How to implement:

To implement dollar-cost averaging, the investor can set up an automatic investment plan with their brokerage or investment company. They can choose how much money they want to invest and how often they want to invest. For example, they could invest $500 every month in a mutual fund or exchange-traded fund (ETF).

Value Investing

Value investing is an investment strategy that involves identifying undervalued stocks and purchasing them at a discounted price. The goal is to find stocks that are trading at a price lower than their intrinsic value. The investor then holds onto the stock until its price rises to its fair value or beyond.

Pros:

- Can lead to significant returns if the undervalued stock performs well

- Provides a margin of safety for the investor, as they are buying at a discounted price
- Encourages a long-term perspective on investing

Cons:

- Requires significant research and analysis to identify undervalued stocks
- Can take a long time for the undervalued stock to reach its fair value
- Can be difficult to determine the intrinsic value of a stock

How to implement:

To implement value investing, the investor must research and analyze different stocks to identify those that are undervalued. They can use various tools and techniques, such as financial ratios, discounted cash flow analysis, and price-to-earnings ratios. Once they have identified an undervalued stock, they can purchase it at a discounted price and hold onto it until its price rises to its fair value or beyond.

Diversification

It is an investment strategy that involves spreading investments across different asset classes, sectors, and geographies to reduce risk. The goal is to create a portfolio that is not heavily concentrated in any one investment or sector. By diversifying, the investor can reduce the impact of market fluctuations on their portfolio.

Pros:

- Reduces the risk of investing in any one investment or sector

- Can provide a more stable return over the long term
- Allows the investor to take advantage of different investment opportunities

Cons:

- Can limit potential returns if one asset class or sector outperforms others
- Requires ongoing monitoring and rebalancing of the portfolio
- Can result in higher transaction costs due to the need to purchase multiple investments

How to implement:

To implement diversification, the investor can create a portfolio that includes a mix of stocks, bonds, real estate, and other asset classes. They can also diversify within each asset class by investing in different sectors

There are many other investment strategies beyond dollar-cost averaging, value investing, and diversification. Some of these include:

1. Growth Investing: This strategy involves investing in companies that are expected to grow faster than the overall market. The focus is on companies that have the potential for strong revenue and earnings growth, even if they have high price-to-earnings ratios.
2. Income Investing: Income investing involves investing in assets that generate regular income, such as dividend-paying stocks, bonds, and real estate investment trusts (REITs). The focus is on generating a steady stream of income rather than capital appreciation.

3. Index Investing: Index investing involves investing in a diversified portfolio of stocks or bonds that tracks a market index, such as the S&P 500 or the Russell 2000. The focus is on achieving returns that are similar to the overall market.

4. Sector Investing: Sector investing involves investing in a specific sector or industry, such as technology or healthcare. The focus is on capitalizing on trends and developments within that particular sector.

5. Market Timing: Market timing involves attempting to predict when the market will go up or down and adjusting your investment strategy accordingly. This strategy is difficult to execute successfully and can be risky.

6. Alternative Investing: Alternative investments include investments in assets such as private equity, hedge funds, and commodities. These investments can offer diversification and potentially higher returns, but also come with higher risk and may require a higher minimum investment.

It's important to note that each investment strategy has its own risks and potential rewards, and what works best for one investor may not work for another. It's important to do your research and seek professional advice before making any investment decisions.

V How to Get Started with Investing

Investing can be a valuable tool for building wealth and achieving financial goals, but it can also be intimidating for beginners. In this section, we will explore the practical steps to start investing, including how to open a brokerage account, choose investments, and place orders.

1. Choose a Brokerage Account

The first step to start investing is to choose a brokerage account. A brokerage account is an investment account that allows you to buy and sell securities, such as stocks, bonds, mutual funds, and ETFs. There are two main types of brokerage accounts: full-service and discount. Full-service brokerages offer a wide range of services, such as investment advice, research, and portfolio management, but they also charge higher fees. Discount brokerages, on the other hand, offer lower fees and commissions but provide fewer services.

When choosing a brokerage account, consider the fees, commissions, minimum investment requirements, and the selection of investment options. Some popular online brokerages include Vanguard, Fidelity, Charles Schwab, and Robinhood.

2. Choose Investments

Once you have opened a brokerage account, the next step is to choose investments. The investment options available to you will depend on your brokerage account and your investment goals. Some common investment options include:

- Stocks: Shares of ownership in a company that trades on stock exchanges. Stocks can be a good choice for investors who want to earn higher returns but are willing to take on more risk.
- Bonds: A type of debt security that pays interest to investors. Bonds can be a good choice for investors who want a more stable source of income but are willing to accept lower returns.
- Mutual Funds: A collection of stocks, bonds, or other securities managed by an investment company. Mutual funds can be

a good choice for investors who want a diversified portfolio but do not have the time or expertise to manage individual investments.

- ETFs: Similar to mutual funds, but trade like stocks on stock exchanges. ETFs can be a good choice for investors who want a diversified portfolio with lower fees than mutual funds.

When choosing investments, consider your investment goals, risk tolerance, and time horizon. It's also important to do your research and understand the potential risks and rewards of each investment option.

3. Place Orders

Once you have chosen your investments, the next step is to place orders. There are two main types of orders: market orders and limit orders. A market order is an order to buy or sell a security at the current market price. A limit order is an order to buy or sell a security at a specific price or better.

When placing orders, consider the fees and commissions associated with each order type. It's also important to monitor your investments regularly and make adjustments as needed.

4. Costs of Investing

Investing comes with costs, such as commissions, fees, and taxes. Commissions are fees charged by brokerage firms for executing trades. Fees can include account maintenance fees, annual fees, and transaction fees. Taxes are also a consideration, as investments may be subject to capital gains taxes or other taxes depending on the investment type and your tax bracket.

When investing, it's important to understand the costs involved and choose investments that align with your budget and financial goals.

5. Avoiding Common Mistakes

Starting to invest can be overwhelming, and there are common mistakes that many beginners make.

Some common mistakes include:

1. **Failing to do research:** It's important to understand the potential risks and rewards of each investment option and do your research before investing.
2. **Focusing on short-term gains:** Investing should be a long-term strategy, and focusing on short-term gains can lead to impulsive decisions and losses.
3. **Not diversifying:** Diversification is important to reduce risk and ensure a balanced portfolio.
4. **Timing the market:** Trying to time the market by buying and selling at the "right" time is a mistake. It's impossible to predict the market with accuracy, and trying to do so can lead to missed opportunities and losses.
5. **Investing with emotions:** Making investment decisions based on emotions, such as fear or greed, can lead to poor decision-making and result in losses. It's important to approach investing with a rational and disciplined mindset.
6. **Not considering taxes:** Taxes can significantly impact investment returns, so it's important to consider the tax implications of investments and make decisions accordingly.

7. **Overconfidence:** Overconfidence can lead to excessive risk-taking and poor decision-making. It's important to approach investing with a humble and realistic mindset.

Tips for avoiding these mistakes include staying disciplined, sticking to a long-term investment plan, regularly reviewing and rebalancing your portfolio, and seeking professional advice if needed.

Finally, it's important to remember that investing is a journey, not a destination. It takes time, patience, and discipline to achieve investment success. But by starting early, setting goals, choosing a strategy, and avoiding common mistakes, anyone can become a successful investor.

VI Investing and Risk Management

Investing always involves risk, and it's important to understand the different types of risks that are associated with investing. Some of the most common risks include market risk, inflation risk, and liquidity risk.

Market risk is the risk of losing money due to changes in the overall market, such as a stock market crash. This type of risk can be managed through diversification, which involves spreading your investments across different types of assets to reduce the impact of any one investment.

Inflation risk is the risk of losing purchasing power over time due to inflation. This can be managed by investing in assets that have historically kept up with inflation, such as stocks, real estate, and commodities.

Liquidity risk is the risk of not being able to sell an investment when you need to. This can be managed by investing in assets that are easily sold, such as stocks and bonds, and by maintaining a diversified portfolio.

To manage these risks, it's important to employ different techniques, such as diversification and asset allocation. Diversification involves investing in a variety of assets, such as stocks, bonds, and real estate, to spread risk and minimize the impact of any one investment. Asset allocation involves determining the right mix of assets for your investment goals, risk tolerance, and time horizon.

Balancing risk and reward is key when investing. Generally, investments that offer higher potential returns come with higher risk. For example, stocks have historically offered higher returns than bonds, but they also come with greater risk. It's important to understand your risk tolerance and invest accordingly, balancing the potential for higher returns with the need to manage risk.

Here are some other types of risk associated with investing:

1. Credit risk: This is the risk that the borrower will not be able to repay their debts, resulting in a loss of principal and interest payments for the lender.
2. Currency risk: This is the risk of losses due to changes in exchange rates when investing in foreign currencies or foreign assets.

3. Interest rate risk: This is the risk of losses due to changes in interest rates, which can affect the value of investments such as bonds and real estate.
4. Business risk: This is the risk associated with a specific company or industry, such as the risk of bankruptcy or a downturn in the industry.
5. Political risk: This is the risk associated with changes in government policies or instability in a particular country or region, which can affect investments in that area.

In conclusion, investing is an important tool for achieving financial growth and security. By investing wisely, individuals can generate wealth, earn passive income, and beat inflation over time. It is important to understand the different types of investments available, including stocks, bonds, mutual funds, and real estate, and to consider the risks and rewards associated with each. Setting SMART investment goals and developing a sound investment strategy can help individuals achieve their financial goals and manage risk effectively.

When getting started with investing, it is important to open a brokerage account, choose investments, and be aware of the costs associated with investing, such as commissions, fees, and taxes. Additionally, it is important to avoid common mistakes such as timing the market and not diversifying one's portfolio. By managing risks through diversification, asset allocation, and other techniques, investors can balance risk and reward to achieve their financial goals.

In summary, the benefits of investing are significant, and with the right knowledge and strategy, anyone can start investing and achieve financial success. It is never too early or too late to start investing, and by taking the necessary steps to get started, individuals can set themselves on a path towards financial security and prosperity.

"Congratulations, you have made significant progress towards achieving financial freedom. To reach your goal fully, I recommend completing the remaining chapters by following sound financial practices such as budgeting, reducing expenses, saving regularly, investing wisely, paying off debt, creating multiple streams of income, and maintaining discipline in managing your finances."

CHAPTER 6

BUILDING PASSIVE INCOME: STRATEGIES FOR BUILDING PASSIVE INCOME STREAMS TO ACHIEVE FINANCIAL FREEDOM

I Introduction

Passive income is the money you earn without actively working for it. It's the result of putting in effort and time upfront to create a source of income that continues to generate revenue long after the initial work is done. Passive income can provide financial freedom, allowing individuals to have more control over their time and work on projects they're passionate about.

This chapter will explore various strategies for building passive income streams and how they can be used to achieve financial freedom.

The key points of the chapter will include:

1. Understanding the importance of passive income
2. Different types of passive income streams
3. Tips for building passive income
4. Examples of successful passive income strategies

By the end of this chapter, readers will have a clear understanding of how to start building passive income and achieving financial freedom.

Understanding Passive Income

Passive income is money earned without actively participating in a job or trade. It is the income generated from assets that require minimal effort to maintain, unlike active income, which is earned from actively working to earn money, such as a regular job.

Passive income can come from various sources, such as rental properties, dividends from stocks, royalties from intellectual property, and interest from investments. Unlike active income, which requires regular effort and time, passive income requires little to no effort once the initial setup is done. This makes passive income a great way to achieve financial freedom and create long-term wealth.

The main difference between passive income and active income is the level of involvement required to earn it. With active income, a person has to exchange their time and labor for payment, while passive income allows a person to earn money without actively participating in the work that generates the income. Understanding the difference between the two is important in building a solid financial plan that includes passive income streams.

Passive income is income earned with little to no effort on the part of the recipient. Unlike active income, which requires you to work for money, passive income generates money without the need for ongoing work.

There are several sources of passive income, including:

1. Rental income: Rental income is money earned by renting out property or real estate. This can include everything from renting out a spare room on Airbnb to owning and renting out an entire apartment building.
2. Dividends: Dividends are payments made by corporations to their shareholders. They are typically paid out on a regular basis and are based on the company's profits.
3. Royalties: Royalties are payments made to a creator for the use of their intellectual property. This can include things like licensing fees for music, books, or software.

4. Investment income: Investment income is money earned through investments such as stocks, bonds, and mutual funds. This income can come from dividends, interest payments, and capital gains.

5. Business income: Business income can be passive if you own a business but have hired someone to manage it for you. In this case, you can earn money without actively working in the business.

These are just a few examples of the many sources of passive income. By diversifying your sources of passive income, you can create a steady stream of income that can help you achieve financial independence and freedom.

II Benefits of Passive Income

Passive income offers a variety of benefits that can help individuals achieve their financial goals and improve their overall quality of life. Some of the key benefits of passive income include:

1. **Financial freedom:** Passive income provides a consistent stream of income that doesn't require active effort or time investment. This allows individuals to achieve financial freedom and potentially retire early.

2. **Time flexibility:** Passive income sources typically require less time and effort than traditional forms of active income, which allows individuals to have more free time to pursue other interests and hobbies.

3. **Increased security:** Having multiple streams of passive income can provide a safety net and protect against unexpected financial setbacks or job loss.

4. **Scalability:** Passive income streams can often be scaled up by investing more time and money into them. For example, if you have a successful rental property, you can buy additional properties and increase your passive income.

5. **Reduced stress:** Passive income can help reduce financial stress, since you have a reliable source of income that doesn't require constant effort or attention.

6. **Retirement income:** Passive income can be an excellent source of retirement income, especially if you build up multiple streams of passive income over time.

7. **Flexibility:** With passive income, you have more flexibility in how you spend your time, since you don't have to be tied to a traditional 9-to-5 job. This can allow you to pursue other interests and hobbies, spend more time with family, or travel more.

8. **Increased creativity:** Having passive income can give you the financial security and freedom to pursue creative endeavors that may not have immediate financial returns. This can lead to personal fulfillment and greater overall happiness.

9. **Opportunity for philanthropy:** With a reliable source of passive income, you may be able to donate more to charitable causes and make a positive impact in the world.

These are just a few of the many benefits of passive income.

Overall, passive income can help individuals achieve greater financial stability and flexibility, while also providing the opportunity for increased personal fulfillment and a better work-life balance. In the following sections, we will explore some of the most effective strategies for building passive income stream

Comparison of passive income to active income and traditional savings methods, such as a savings account or a CD

	Passive Income	**Active Income**	**Traditional Savings Methods**
Definition	Income earned with little to no effort or time investment	Income earned through active work or services provided	Interest earned on savings deposits
Effort Required	Low	High	Low
Time Investment	Minimal	Significant	Minimal
Potential Returns	High	High	Low to Moderate
Risk	Moderate	High	Low
Flexibility	High	Low	Low
Scalability	High	Low	Low
Dependency on Work	No	Yes	No

Passive income offers the potential for higher returns with minimal effort and time investment, while traditional savings methods have low to moderate returns and low risk but require little effort. Active income requires significant effort and time investment but offers the potential for high returns. Additionally, passive income is more flexible and scalable than active income or traditional savings methods and is not dependent on ongoing work or services provided. However, passive income does come with some level of risk, which should be considered when developing a passive income strategy.

III Types of Passive Income

Passive income can be earned in many different ways, from investments to rental income. In this section, we will explore some of the most common types of passive income:

1. **Rental income:** Rental income is one of the most popular forms of passive income. It involves owning a property and renting it out to tenants. This can include both residential and commercial properties. Rental income can be a great way to generate regular income without a lot of effort, but it does come with some risks and responsibilities.

2. **Dividend income:** Dividend income is earned by owning stocks that pay dividends to their shareholders. Dividends are typically paid out quarterly, and the amount you receive will depend on the number of shares you own and the dividend yield of the stock. Dividend income can be a reliable source of passive income, but it does require some knowledge of the stock market.

3. **Interest income:** Interest income is earned by investing in bonds or other fixed-income securities. When you buy a bond, you are essentially lending money to the issuer and receiving interest payments in return. Interest income can be a good

way to generate regular income with a lower level of risk than other types of investments.

4. **Capital gains:** Capital gains are earned by buying and selling assets such as stocks, real estate, or businesses. When you sell an asset for more than you paid for it, you realize a capital gain. Capital gains can be a great way to generate passive income, but they do require a certain level of knowledge and expertise.

Here is a table comparing the different types of passive income to active income and traditional savings methods:

Type of Income	Definition	Advantages	Disadvantages
Passive Income	Income earned without active involvement	Potential for high returns with minimal effort	Can require a significant initial investment
Active Income	Income earned through work or employment	Reliable source of income	Limited earning potential
Savings Accounts	Interest earned on cash deposits	Safe and low-risk	Low returns
Certificates of Deposit (CDs)	Interest earned on fixed-term deposits	Safe and low-risk	Locked-in funds with limited access and low returns

Overall, passive income can be a great way to generate regular income and achieve financial freedom. By understanding the different types of passive income and the advantages and disadvantages of each, you can make informed decisions about how to invest your money and build your passive income streams.

Explanation of the risks and rewards of each type of passive income

Passive Income Type	Rewards	Risks
Rental Income	Provides ongoing monthly cash flow and potential long-term appreciation of property value	Property damage, vacancy periods, difficult tenants, potential liability issues
Dividend Income	Regular payments from profitable companies, potential for dividend growth over time	Fluctuation in stock prices, potential for companies to cut or eliminate dividends
Interest Income	Guaranteed return on investment, low risk	Low interest rates, inflation, potential for default on loans
Capital Gains	Profit from the sale of assets, potential for high returns	Market fluctuations, potential for high capital gains taxes

Note that this is just an example, and there may be other risks and rewards associated with each type of passive income depending on the specific investment. It's important to carefully research and evaluate any potential investment before committing any funds.

IV Building Passive Income Streams

Passive income is a powerful tool for achieving financial freedom and creating long-term wealth. There are many different strategies for building passive income streams, each with its own advantages and challenges. In this chapter, we will explore some of the most effective strategies for building passive income and provide practical tips for getting started.

1. Investing in Dividend-Paying Stocks

Dividend-paying stocks are a popular way to generate passive income. Dividends are payments made by a company to its shareholders, usually on a quarterly basis. By investing in stocks that pay dividends, you can earn regular income without having to sell your shares. Some stocks have a higher dividend yield than others, which means they pay a higher percentage of their share price in dividends.

One key advantage of dividend-paying stocks is that they can provide a reliable source of income over time. However, it's important to remember that stock prices can be volatile, and dividends are not guaranteed. To reduce risk, it's important to diversify your portfolio and invest in a mix of dividend-paying stocks across different industries and sectors.

2. Real Estate Investing

Real estate is another popular way to generate passive income. Rental properties can provide a steady stream of rental income, while also appreciating in value over time. There are a few different ways to invest in real estate, including purchasing rental properties, investing in real estate investment trusts (REITs), and using crowdfunding platforms to invest in real estate projects.

One advantage of real estate investing is that it can provide a reliable source of passive income, particularly if you invest in rental properties in high-demand areas. However, real estate investing can also be risky, and it's important to do your due diligence before making any investments.

3. Creating Digital Products

In today's digital age, creating digital products is an increasingly popular way to generate passive income. Digital products can include e-books, online courses, and software products, among others. Once you create a digital product, you can sell it online and earn passive income without having to invest more time or resources.

One key advantage of creating digital products is that there are virtually no overhead costs, which means you can earn a high profit margin on each sale. However, creating a successful digital product can be challenging, and it's important to invest time and resources into marketing and promoting your product to ensure that it reaches its target audience.

In conclusion, building passive income streams can be a powerful way to achieve financial freedom and create long-term wealth. By investing in dividend-paying stocks, real estate, and creating digital products, you can generate reliable sources of passive income that can help you achieve your financial goals. However, it's important to remember that building passive income takes time, effort, and a willingness to take risks. With the right strategies and a commitment to your goals, however, anyone can build a successful passive income stream.

Aspect	Explanation
Research	Conducting thorough research on potential passive income streams, such as analyzing market trends, evaluating investment opportunities, and understanding the risks involved.
Planning	Developing a clear plan for building passive income, including setting realistic goals, determining investment amounts and timelines, and monitoring progress.
Diversification	Spreading investments across multiple passive income streams to reduce risk and maximize potential returns, such as investing in a mix of dividend-paying stocks, rental properties, and digital products.

V Maximizing Passive Income

Passive income can be a powerful tool for achieving financial freedom, but it's important to maximize its potential. Here are some tips for getting the most out of your passive income streams:

1. **Reinvest profits:** One of the best ways to maximize passive income is to reinvest your profits. Whether it's buying more dividend-paying stocks or purchasing additional rental properties, reinvesting your earnings can help your passive income grow exponentially over time.

2. **Reduce expenses:** Another way to maximize passive income is to reduce expenses associated with your investments. For example, if you're a real estate investor, you may be able to

negotiate lower property management fees or find ways to cut costs on repairs and maintenance.

3. **Optimize tax strategies:** Taxes can eat into your passive income, so it's important to optimize your tax strategies. This might include setting up a pass-through entity for your rental properties, taking advantage of tax-deferred retirement accounts, or working with a tax professional to identify other deductions and credits.

4. **Focus on high-yield opportunities:** When building your passive income streams, it's important to focus on high-yield opportunities that offer a good return on investment. This might mean seeking out dividend-paying stocks with high yields or investing in properties that have the potential to generate significant rental income.

5. **Diversify your portfolio:** Diversification is key to minimizing risk and maximizing returns. When building your passive income streams, it's important to diversify across different asset classes, such as stocks, real estate, and bonds.

By following these tips, you can maximize the potential of your passive income streams and achieve financial freedom faster.

Here are some real-life examples of successful passive income earners and their strategies:

1. Pat Flynn: Pat Flynn is a successful online entrepreneur and podcaster who has built multiple streams of passive income. His primary source of passive income is through his website, Smart Passive Income, where he earns money through affiliate marketing, sponsorships, and digital products.

2. Dividend Growth Investor: Dividend Growth Investor is an anonymous blogger who has built a significant passive income stream through dividend investing. He invests in high-quality dividend-paying stocks and reinvests the dividends to compound his returns.

3. Paula Pant: Paula Pant is a real estate investor and blogger who has built a successful passive income stream through rental properties. She owns several rental properties and earns passive income from rental payments each month.

4. Michelle Schroeder-Gardner: Michelle Schroeder-Gardner is a successful blogger and affiliate marketer who has built multiple streams of passive income. She earns passive income through affiliate marketing, sponsorships, and digital products.

5. Jeff Rose: Jeff Rose is a financial advisor and blogger who has built a successful passive income stream through a combination of dividend investing, real estate investing, and online businesses. He also earns passive income through book sales and affiliate marketing.

These successful passive income earners have different strategies for building and maximizing their passive income streams. However, they all have in common a focus on building diversified income streams, researching their investments carefully, and continually reinvesting their profits to grow their income over time.

VI Overcoming Obstacles to Passive Income

Passive income streams can provide a steady source of income and financial stability, but they are not without their challenges.

In this chapter, we will discuss the common obstacles to building passive income and strategies for overcoming them.

Lack of Capital

1. One of the most significant obstacles to building passive income is a lack of capital. Many passive income streams require a significant upfront investment, such as real estate investing or buying dividend-paying stocks. If you don't have the capital to invest, you can consider other strategies such as creating digital products or starting a side business that requires minimal upfront investment.

Market Volatility

2. Another obstacle to building passive income is market volatility. Some passive income streams, such as stocks or mutual funds, are subject to market fluctuations that can impact your earnings. To overcome this obstacle, it's important to diversify your investments across different asset classes and industries. This way, if one industry or asset class experiences a downturn, your overall portfolio will not be as affected.

Legal Issues

3. Finally, legal issues can also be a significant obstacle to building passive income. For example, rental income streams can be impacted by tenant disputes or legal issues. To overcome this obstacle, it's essential to understand the legal requirements for your passive income streams and ensure that you have proper documentation and legal representation if necessary.

Overall, while there are obstacles to building passive income, they can be overcome with proper planning and strategy. By diversifying your investments, creating a sustainable passive income portfolio, and seeking legal advice if necessary, you can overcome the obstacles and achieve financial stability through passive income.

In conclusion, passive income is an essential component of achieving financial freedom and security. It provides individuals with the opportunity to generate income streams without actively working for them. Understanding the differences between passive and active income is crucial in developing an effective strategy for building passive income streams. The benefits of passive income, including financial freedom, time flexibility, and increased security, are significant and should not be overlooked.

To build passive income streams, individuals need to research and plan their investment strategy carefully. Diversification is important in reducing risk and maximizing returns. Real estate investing, dividend-paying stocks, and creating digital products are some of the most popular strategies for building a passive income.

Maximizing passive income requires a focus on reinvesting profits, reducing expenses, and optimizing tax strategies. Successful passive income earners have developed effective strategies that have led to significant financial gains.

Overcoming common obstacles to building passive income, such as lack of capital or market volatility, requires perseverance and a willingness to adapt to changing circumstances.

In conclusion, building passive income streams is a powerful tool for achieving financial freedom and security. By understanding the various types of passive income, developing effective strategies, and overcoming obstacles, individuals can build sustainable passive income portfolios that provide long-term financial benefits.

CHAPTER - 7

DEBT MANAGEMENT

Debt is an unavoidable part of modern life, and while it can be a useful tool for achieving financial goals, it can also be a burden that holds us back from achieving true financial freedom. Whether it's credit card debt, student loans, a mortgage, or a car loan, most of us will have to deal with debt at some point in our lives. But how we manage that debt can make all the difference in our financial wellbeing.

In this chapter, we'll explore the different types of debt and the strategies for paying it off and avoiding debt traps. We'll discuss the benefits of debt management, such as improved credit scores, reduced stress, and increased financial security. We'll also provide practical examples and tips for developing a debt management plan that works for your unique situation.

By the end of this chapter, you'll have a better understanding of how to manage your debt effectively and take control of your financial future.

Definition of debt and the different types of debt, such as credit card debt, student loans, and mortgages

Debt can be defined as an amount of money borrowed by an individual or organization from a lender with the agreement to pay it back over time with interest. There are various types of debt, including:

1. Credit card debt: This is a type of debt that is accumulated by using credit cards to purchase goods or services. The balance is carried over from one month to the next, and interest is charged on the unpaid balance.

2. Student loans: These are loans that are taken out to pay for education expenses such as tuition, room, and board, textbooks, and other related expenses. Student loans can be taken out from the government or private lenders.
3. Mortgages: This is a type of loan used to purchase a home. The home is used as collateral for the loan, and the borrower agrees to make monthly payments until the loan is paid off in full.
4. Personal loans: These are loans that are taken out for personal expenses such as home improvements, medical bills, or other unexpected expenses.
5. Auto loans: These are loans that are taken out to purchase a vehicle. The vehicle is used as collateral for the loan, and the borrower agrees to make monthly payments until the loan is paid off in full.

Understanding the different types of debt is important because each type of debt comes with its own terms and conditions, including interest rates, repayment schedules, and penalties for late payments. It is essential to carefully consider the terms of each loan before borrowing to ensure that you can comfortably make the required payments.

the consequences of carrying high levels of debt, such as reduced credit score and financial stress

Consequence	Explanation
Reduced credit score	High levels of debt can cause your credit score to decrease, making it harder to qualify for loans or credit cards with favorable terms in the future.
Financial stress	Carrying high levels of debt can lead to financial stress, which can affect your mental health, relationships, and overall well-being. It can also lead to difficulties in meeting monthly payments and making ends meet.
Increased interest payments	The more debt you have, the more interest you'll have to pay, which can significantly increase the overall cost of your debt.
Limited financial options	High levels of debt can limit your financial options, making it difficult to save for the future or invest in opportunities that could improve your financial situation.
Risk of default	If you're unable to make your debt payments, you risk defaulting on your loans, which can lead to legal action, collection calls, and damage to your credit score.

Note that this table is not exhaustive and other consequences may exist depending on the specific type and amount of debt.

Strategies for Paying Off Debt

Effective debt management requires a solid plan for paying off outstanding balances. This chapter will provide an overview of different strategies that individuals can use to pay off their debts.

A. The Debt Snowball Method

The debt snowball method is a popular debt reduction strategy that involves paying off debts in order from smallest to largest. This method involves making minimum payments on all debts except for the smallest one, on which the debtor should focus all available funds. Once the smallest debt is paid off, the debtor should move on to the next smallest debt, and so on, until all debts are paid off.

The advantage of the debt snowball method is that it provides a sense of accomplishment and motivation as the debtor sees the number of debts decreasing. However, this method may not be the most financially efficient, as it does not take into account the interest rates on the debts.

B. The Debt Avalanche Method

The debt avalanche method is another popular debt reduction strategy that involves paying off debts in order of interest rate, from highest to lowest. This method involves making minimum payments on all debts except for the one with the highest interest rate, on which the debtor should focus all available funds. Once the debt with the highest interest rate is paid off, the debtor should move on to the next debt with the highest interest rate, and so on, until all debts are paid off.

The advantage of the debt avalanche method is that it saves the debtor the most money in interest payments over the long term. However, it may be less motivating than the debt snowball method, as it may take longer to pay off the first debt.

C. Debt Consolidation

Debt consolidation involves combining multiple debts into a single loan with a lower interest rate. This can make it easier to manage payments and can also reduce the amount of interest paid over time. Debt consolidation can be done through a balance transfer credit card, a personal loan, or a home equity loan.

The advantage of debt consolidation is that it simplifies debt repayment and can save money on interest. However, it is important to be cautious when considering debt consolidation, as it can lead to additional fees and may not always result in lower overall payments.

D. Other Strategies

Other strategies for paying off debt include increasing income through a side hustle or second job, negotiating with creditors for lower interest rates or payment plans, and seeking the help of a credit counseling service.

It is important to choose a debt repayment strategy that works best for each individual's financial situation and personal preferences. It is also important to stay committed to the chosen strategy and to seek professional advice if needed. With determination and discipline, it is possible to become debt-free and achieve financial freedom.

The benefits and drawbacks of each strategy with examples

Strategy	Benefits	Drawbacks
Debt snowball method	- Provides motivation by targeting smallest debts first.	- May not be the most financially efficient method.- Interest rates may vary across debts.
Debt avalanche method	- Can save more money in the long run by targeting debts with highest interest rates first.	- May take longer to see progress since highest interest rate debts may also be the largest debts.

Debt consolidation	- Combines multiple debts into one payment. - May be able to negotiate a lower interest rate. 	- May result in a longer payment term, resulting in more interest paid overall. May require collateral.

Note: This table is just an example and may not include all possible benefits and drawbacks for each strategy. It's important to do your own research and consider your individual financial situation before deciding on a debt payoff strategy.

Avoiding Debt Traps

Debt can be a slippery slope, and many people find themselves falling into debt traps that can be difficult to climb out of. In this chapter, we'll discuss some common debt traps and how to avoid them.

Payday loans

1. Payday loans are a type of short-term loan that typically has very high interest rates and fees. These loans are often marketed to people who are in a tight financial situation and need cash quickly. However, they can be very expensive and can lead to a cycle of debt that is difficult to escape. The best way to avoid payday loans is to have an emergency fund in place so that you don't need to rely on them in a financial emergency.

High-interest credit cards

2. Credit cards can be a useful tool for managing your finances, but they can also be a trap if you're not careful. High-interest credit cards can quickly spiral out of control if you don't pay off the balance in full each month. To avoid falling into this

trap, try to only use your credit card for purchases you can pay off in full each month, and make a plan to pay off any existing high-interest debt as soon as possible.

Predatory lending practices

3. Predatory lending practices are when lenders take advantage of people who are in a vulnerable financial situation. This can include things like high-interest loans, hidden fees, and aggressive collection tactics. To avoid these practices, make sure you do your research and choose reputable lenders. If you're unsure about a lender, it's always a good idea to seek advice from a financial advisor or credit counseling service.

By being aware of these common debt traps and taking steps to avoid them, you can put yourself in a better position to manage your debt and achieve financial stability.

Strategies for avoiding debt traps,

Common Debt Traps	Strategies for Avoiding
Payday loans	Create a budget to track expenses and income, and avoid taking out high-interest loans
High-interest credit cards	Pay off credit card balances in full each month, or consider using a lower-interest alternative like a personal loan
Predatory lending practices	Research and compare lenders before taking out a loan, and seek financial advice from a trusted professional

Overspending	Set financial goals and priorities, avoid impulse buying, and track expenses to stay within budget
Lack of emergency fund	Build an emergency fund to cover unexpected expenses and avoid taking on debt to pay for them

Balancing Debt Management and Saving for the Future

Managing debt effectively is important, but so is planning for the future. It's essential to find a balance between paying off debt and saving for long-term financial goals. Here are some key considerations:

1. Prioritize high-interest debt: If you have multiple debts, prioritize paying off the ones with the highest interest rates first. This will help you save money on interest charges and reduce your debt faster.

2. Create a budget: To balance debt repayment with saving, it's important to create a budget that allocates funds for both. Start by tracking your income and expenses, then identify areas where you can cut back and redirect those funds towards debt repayment and savings.

3. Build an emergency fund: Unexpected expenses can derail your debt repayment plan, so it's important to have a safety net in place. Aim to save at least three to six months' worth of living expenses in an emergency fund. This will help you avoid taking on more debt in case of a financial setback.

4. Contribute to retirement savings: Even if you're carrying debt, it's important to contribute to retirement savings. Take advantage of any employer-sponsored plans, such as 401(k)s

or IRAs, and consider automating your contributions to make it easier to save consistently.

5. Consider refinancing: If you have high-interest debt, refinancing can help you lower your interest rate and save money over time. This is especially true for student loans or mortgages, where a small reduction in interest rate can translate into significant savings over the life of the loan.

Balancing debt management with saving for the future can be challenging, but it's essential for long-term financial success. By prioritizing high-interest debt, creating a budget, building an emergency fund, contributing to retirement savings, and considering refinancing options, you can achieve a healthy balance between debt repayment and saving.

Here are some strategies for prioritizing debt repayment while still saving for the future:

1. Create a budget: By creating a budget, you can identify areas where you can cut back on expenses and redirect those funds towards debt repayment and savings.

2. Pay yourself first: Make sure to set aside a portion of your income for savings and contribute to your retirement fund before allocating funds towards debt repayment. This way, you are building a safety net for the future while also tackling your debt.

3. Focus on high-interest debt: Prioritize paying off high-interest debt first, such as credit card debt, before allocating funds towards lower-interest debt.

4. Consider balance transfer credit cards: If you have high-interest credit card debt, consider transferring the balance to

a card with a lower interest rate. This can help you save on interest and pay off your debt faster.

5. Negotiate with lenders: If you are struggling to make your debt payments, consider reaching out to your lenders to negotiate a repayment plan that works for you. This can help you avoid defaulting on your debt and damaging your credit score.

6. Look for ways to increase income: Consider taking on a side job or selling unused items to generate extra income that can be used towards debt repayment and savings.

Remember, finding the right balance between debt repayment and saving for the future will depend on your individual financial situation. It's important to regularly review your budget and adjust your strategy as needed.

Managing Debt in Challenging Times

Dealing with debt can be challenging at any time, but it becomes even more difficult during tough economic times. This chapter will focus on strategies for managing debt during challenging times, such as job loss or a financial crisis.

When faced with a difficult financial situation, it's important to prioritize your expenses and make a plan for managing your debt. Here are some tips for managing debt during challenging times:

1. Cut Back on Expenses: During difficult times, it's important to cut back on non-essential expenses to free up more money to pay down debt. This might mean canceling subscriptions or memberships, reducing dining out, and finding ways to reduce your utility bills.

2. Seek Financial Assistance: There are many financial assistance programs available to people who are struggling with debt during challenging times. For example, some credit card companies offer hardship programs that allow you to temporarily suspend payments or reduce interest rates. You can also seek out government assistance programs or contact a non-profit credit counseling agency for help.

3. Consider Debt Consolidation: If you have multiple debts with high-interest rates, debt consolidation may be a good option. Debt consolidation involves taking out a single loan to pay off all of your other debts, leaving you with one manageable monthly payment.

4. Prioritize Debt Payments: If you're unable to pay all of your debts, it's important to prioritize your payments. Focus on paying off high-interest debt first, as it's costing you the most money in interest charges. You may also want to consider negotiating with your creditors to see if you can get a lower interest rate or a more manageable payment plan.

5. Build Up Your Emergency Fund: Having an emergency fund can help you avoid going into debt during challenging times. Aim to save up enough money to cover at least 3-6 months of your living expenses.

In conclusion, managing debt during challenging times can be difficult, but it's not impossible. By cutting back on expenses, seeking financial assistance, considering debt consolidation, prioritizing debt payments, and building up your emergency fund, you can work towards becoming debt-free even during tough economic times.

During challenging times, such as job loss or a financial crisis, managing debt can become even more difficult. It's important to have a plan in place to avoid defaulting on loans or accumulating more debt.

One strategy is to negotiate with creditors. Contacting your lenders and explaining your situation may allow you to work out a modified payment plan or even have some debt forgiven. This can help alleviate some financial pressure and keep you from falling behind on payments.

Another strategy is to seek financial assistance from non-profit organizations, such as credit counseling agencies or local government agencies. These organizations may offer free or low-cost assistance with budgeting, debt management, and other financial issues.

Finally, seeking professional help from a financial advisor or attorney may be necessary in some situations. They can provide guidance on how to navigate your finances during difficult times and help you make informed decisions about managing your debt.

It's important to remember that managing debt during challenging times requires a proactive approach. Don't wait until you're already in trouble to start seeking assistance. Stay on top of your finances and have a plan in place for how to handle unexpected situations.

In summary, managing debt is a crucial component of achieving financial success. In this article, we have covered several key points, including the importance of tracking and understanding your debts, creating a budget and sticking to it, prioritizing high-interest debts, and considering consolidation or refinancing options.

It's essential to prioritize debt management and take steps towards becoming debt-free. This can include making larger payments than the minimum required, avoiding new debt, and seeking professional assistance if necessary.

Ultimately, achieving financial success requires discipline, patience, and a long-term mindset. By focusing on effective debt management, you can lay the foundation for a healthier and more prosperous financial future. Remember to stay committed to your goals, stay motivated, and always be willing to adjust your strategy if necessary.

Remember this 10 Key points about Debt Management:

1. Managing debt is an essential component of achieving financial success.
2. Understanding and tracking your debts is crucial for effective debt management.
3. Creating and sticking to a budget is an important part of debt management.
4. Prioritizing high-interest debts can help you pay off your debts faster.
5. Consolidation or refinancing can be viable options for managing debt.
6. Making larger payments than the minimum required can help you pay off debts faster.
7. Avoiding new debt is crucial to achieving debt management goals.

8. Seeking professional assistance may be necessary for some individuals.
9. Discipline, patience, and a long-term mindset are required to achieve financial success.
10. Staying committed to goals, staying motivated, and adjusting strategies as needed are all critical elements of effective debt management.

CHAPTER-8

RETIREMENT PLANNING

I. Introduction

Retirement planning is the process of setting financial and lifestyle goals for retirement and taking steps to achieve those goals. It involves determining how much money you will need to live comfortably in retirement and creating a savings and investment plan to help you achieve that goal.

Retirement planning is important because it allows you to ensure a comfortable and secure retirement. As people are living longer than ever before, retirement can last for several decades. Without proper planning, retirees risk running out of money and not being able to maintain their desired lifestyle.

Moreover, with the decline of traditional pensions, individuals are now largely responsible for saving and investing for their own retirement. Therefore, having a solid retirement plan is essential to secure your financial future and maintain a comfortable standard of living in retirement. In short, retirement planning is critical to ensure that you have the financial resources to enjoy a fulfilling and stress-free retirement.

Retirement planning is not without its challenges. Some of the key challenges that individuals face in retirement planning include:

1. Increasing life expectancy: As people are living longer than ever before, the challenge of funding a longer retirement period has become more significant. This requires individuals to plan and save for a longer retirement horizon, which may require different investment strategies and asset allocation.

2. Changing economic conditions: Economic conditions, such as inflation, interest rates, and market volatility, can significantly impact retirement savings and investment strategies. Moreover, economic changes can also impact Social Security and pension benefits, making it essential to monitor and adjust retirement plans accordingly

3. Healthcare costs: Healthcare costs are a significant expense in retirement, and they are rising at a faster rate than inflation. Planning for healthcare expenses is critical to ensure that retirees can afford the care they need.

4. Savings shortfall: Many individuals are not saving enough for retirement, which can be due to various reasons such as inadequate income, lack of access to employer-sponsored retirement plans, or poor financial habits. This shortfall can make it challenging to achieve retirement goals and may require more aggressive savings and investment strategies

5. Changing retirement landscape: Retirement is evolving, and the traditional pension plans are being replaced by defined-contribution plans, such as 401(k)s. This shift has made individuals more responsible for their retirement savings and investment strategies, making it essential to stay informed and seek professional advice when needed.

In summary, retirement planning is challenging due to various factors such as increasing life expectancy, changing economic conditions, rising healthcare costs, savings shortfalls, and the evolving retirement landscape. It's crucial to consider these challenges while creating a retirement plan and seek professional advice when needed to ensure that your retirement goals are met.

Follow these steps:

1. Estimate retirement expenses: Estimate your expected retirement expenses, including housing, healthcare, food, transportation, travel, and entertainment.
2. Consider inflation: Inflation can significantly impact retirement expenses, so it's essential to consider this when estimating expenses.
3. Assess current savings and investments: Determine how much you currently have saved and invested for retirement.
4. Determine retirement income sources: Identify potential sources of retirement income, such as Social Security, pensions, and retirement savings.
5. Determine the retirement savings gap: Compare estimated expenses and retirement income sources to determine how much additional savings are needed to meet retirement goals.
6. Adjust goals as needed: Review and adjust retirement goals regularly as circumstances change, such as changes in health, lifestyle, or financial situation.

setting retirement goals is critical to creating a solid retirement plan. Individuals should consider retirement age, lifestyle expectations, and financial needs when determining their retirement goals. By following the steps above, individuals can set realistic retirement goals and adjust them as needed to achieve their desired retirement lifestyle.

II The importance of considering factors such as inflation, healthcare costs, and unexpected expenses

When setting retirement goals and planning for retirement, it's essential to consider various factors that can significantly impact retirement savings and expenses. Some of the most critical factors to consider include inflation, healthcare costs, and unexpected expenses.

1. Inflation: Inflation can significantly impact retirement savings and expenses. Over time, the cost of goods and services tends to increase due to inflation, reducing the purchasing power of retirement savings. Therefore, it's crucial to account for inflation when setting retirement goals and planning for retirement.

2. Healthcare Costs: Healthcare expenses are one of the most significant expenses in retirement. Healthcare costs tend to increase at a faster rate than inflation, making it critical to account for these expenses in retirement planning. Individuals should consider the cost of Medicare premiums, supplemental insurance, long-term care insurance, and out-of-pocket healthcare expenses when setting retirement goals.

3. Unexpected Expenses: Unexpected expenses, such as home repairs, car repairs, and medical emergencies, can significantly impact retirement savings and expenses. Therefore, it's essential to set aside emergency funds to cover unexpected expenses and consider these expenses when setting retirement goals.

Considering these factors is critical to ensure that retirement goals are achievable and that individuals can maintain their desired lifestyle in retirement. Failing to account for inflation, healthcare costs, and unexpected expenses can result in a retirement savings shortfall, reducing the quality of life in retirement. Therefore, individuals should seek professional advice and review their retirement plan regularly to ensure that it remains on track to meet their goals.

III Saving for Retirement

There are various retirement savings options available to individuals, each with its advantages and disadvantages. Below are some of the most common retirement savings options:

1. Employer-Sponsored Plans: Many employers offer retirement savings plans, such as 401(k) and 403(b) plans, to their employees. These plans allow employees to contribute pre-tax income, reducing their taxable income and allowing their retirement savings to grow tax-free until withdrawn in retirement. Some employers also offer matching contributions, which can significantly boost retirement savings. (Please check the scheme details according to the country you live in)

2. Individual Retirement Accounts (IRAs): IRAs are a retirement savings option available to individuals who do not have access to employer-sponsored plans or want to supplement their retirement savings. There are two types of IRAs: traditional and Roth. Traditional IRAs allow individuals to contribute pre-tax income, while Roth IRAs allow individuals to contribute after-tax income. Both types of IRAs offer tax-free growth of retirement savings, with different tax implications upon withdrawal in retirement.

3. Taxable Investment Accounts: Taxable investment accounts are a retirement savings option that allows individuals to invest in stocks, bonds, and other securities outside of a retirement account. While these accounts do not offer tax benefits like employer-sponsored plans or IRAs, they offer more flexibility in terms of investment options and access to funds.

When choosing a retirement savings option, individuals should consider their goals, financial situation, and tax implications. Employer-sponsored plans are a great option for individuals who have access to them, as they often offer matching contributions and tax benefits. IRAs are a good option for individuals who do not have access to employer-sponsored plans or want to supplement their retirement savings. Taxable investment accounts are a good option for individuals who want more flexibility in terms of investment options and access to funds.

Regardless of the retirement savings option chosen, it's essential to save consistently and regularly to achieve retirement goals. Individuals should aim to save at least 10-15% of their income towards retirement savings and review their retirement plan regularly to ensure that it remains on track to meet their goals.

Retirement planning and savings options can vary significantly from country to country, depending on factors such as government policies, cultural attitudes, and economic conditions. Below are some examples of how retirement planning and savings options can differ across different countries:

1. Social Security: In many countries, the government provides a social security system that provides retirement benefits to eligible individuals. The eligibility requirements, benefit levels, and funding mechanisms can vary significantly from country to country.

2. Employer-Sponsored Plans: Employer-sponsored retirement plans, such as 401(k) plans, are common in the United States but less prevalent in other countries. In some countries, employers are required by law to provide retirement benefits to their employees.

3. Mandatory Savings: Some countries have mandatory retirement savings programs, where individuals are required by law to contribute a portion of their income to a retirement savings account. Examples include Australia's superannuation system and Singapore's Central Provident Fund.

4. Investment Options: The types of investment options available for retirement savings can vary from country to country. In some countries, such as the United States, individuals have access to a wide range of investment options through their retirement accounts. In other countries, the investment options may be more limited.

5. Retirement Age: The retirement age can vary from country to country, with some countries allowing individuals to retire earlier or later than others. The retirement age can also be affected by government policies and economic conditions.

Overall, retirement planning and savings options can vary significantly from country to country. Individuals should research the retirement savings options available to them in their country and consider factors such as government policies, cultural attitudes, and economic conditions when making retirement planning decisions. Seeking professional advice can also be helpful in navigating the complexities of retirement planning and savings options in different countries.

How to calculate retirement savings needs and how to determine the appropriate asset allocation based on retirement goals and risk tolerance

Calculating retirement savings needs and determining appropriate asset allocation are essential steps in retirement planning. Below are some tips on how to approach these important aspects of retirement planning:

1. **Calculating Retirement Savings Needs:** To determine how much retirement savings is needed, individuals should consider their desired retirement age, lifestyle expectations, and estimated retirement expenses. It's important to consider factors such as inflation, healthcare costs, and unexpected expenses when estimating retirement expenses. One rule of thumb is to aim for a retirement income that is 70-80% of pre-retirement income. There are also retirement savings calculators available online that can help individuals estimate their retirement savings needs.

2. **Determining Asset Allocation:** Asset allocation refers to the distribution of retirement savings across different types of investments, such as stocks, bonds, and cash. The appropriate asset allocation depends on an individual's retirement goals and risk tolerance. Generally, younger individuals can afford to take on more risk and invest a higher percentage of their retirement savings in stocks, while older individuals may

want to shift towards more conservative investments, such as bonds and cash. A common rule of thumb for determining asset allocation is to subtract an individual's age from 100 and invest that percentage in stocks, with the remainder invested in bonds and cash.

3. **Rebalancing:** Over time, the performance of different types of investments can cause an individual's asset allocation to shift. To maintain an appropriate asset allocation, individuals should periodically rebalance their portfolio. Rebalancing involves selling some investments that have performed well and buying investments that have underperformed to maintain the desired asset allocation.

It's important to note that retirement planning is not a one-time event. Individuals should review and adjust their retirement plan periodically to ensure that it remains on track to meet their retirement goals. Seeking professional advice can also be helpful in determining appropriate retirement savings needs and asset allocation.

Here's an example calculation for retirement savings needs:

Assume John is currently 35 years old and wants to retire at age 65. He currently earns $75,000 per year and expects to need 75% of his pre-retirement income in retirement. He estimates that his retirement expenses will be $50,000 per year in today's dollars, and he expects an average inflation rate of 3% per year.

To calculate John's retirement savings needs, we can use the following formula:

Retirement Savings Needs = (Retirement Expenses / Withdrawal Rate) x (1 + Inflation Rate)^Number of Years in Retirement

In this case, John's retirement savings needs would be:

Retirement Savings Needs = ($50,000 / 0.75) x (1 + 0.03)^30 = $1,982,373

This means that John would need to save approximately $1.98 million by the time he retires at age 65 to generate $50,000 per year in retirement income, adjusted for inflation.

Of course, this is just a simplified example, and individual circumstances can vary widely. It's important to consider a range of factors when estimating retirement savings needs, including expected retirement expenses, inflation, investment returns, and individual risk tolerance.

IV Managing Retirement Investments

Managing retirement investments is an important part of retirement planning. Below are some investment strategies to consider for retirement savings:

1. Diversification: Diversification involves investing in a variety of assets, such as stocks, bonds, and cash, to spread risk across different types of investments. By diversifying their portfolio, investors can potentially reduce the impact of market volatility on their retirement savings. Diversification can also help investors take advantage of different market conditions and investment opportunities.

2. Asset Allocation: Asset allocation refers to the distribution of retirement savings across different types of investments, such as stocks, bonds, and cash. The appropriate asset allocation depends on an individual's retirement goals and risk tolerance. Generally, younger individuals can afford to take on more risk and invest a higher percentage of their retirement savings in stocks, while older individuals may want to shift towards more conservative investments, such as bonds and cash.

3. Rebalancing: Over time, the performance of different types of investments can cause an individual's asset allocation to shift. To maintain an appropriate asset allocation, individuals should periodically rebalance their portfolio. Rebalancing involves selling some investments that have performed well and buying investments that have underperformed to maintain the desired asset allocation.

4. Retirement Income Strategies: As retirement approaches, investors may want to consider transitioning their investment portfolio from growth-oriented investments to more income-generating investments. For example, investors may want to consider investing in dividend-paying stocks or bonds with regular coupon payments. This can provide a steady stream of income in retirement.

5. Professional Advice: Managing retirement investments can be complex, and seeking professional advice can be helpful in determining appropriate investment strategies. A financial advisor can help investors determine an appropriate asset allocation and provide guidance on investment selection and management

6. Monitor Investment Performance: Regularly monitoring investment performance is important to ensure that investments are meeting their expected returns. Investors can use tools such as performance reports, investment statements, and online investment portals to track the performance of their investments.

7. Consider Changes in Personal Circumstances: Changes in personal circumstances, such as a change in employment, a change in family situation, or a change in financial situation, can impact an individual's retirement savings goals and investment strategy. Investors should periodically review their personal circumstances and adjust their investment strategy as needed.

8. Consider Changes in Economic Conditions: Changes in economic conditions, such as interest rate changes, inflation, or market volatility, can impact investment performance. Investors should stay informed about economic conditions and consider adjusting their investment strategy in response.

Overall, monitoring and adjusting investments is an ongoing process that requires regular attention and review. By staying informed about investment performance, personal circumstances, and economic conditions, investors can adjust their investment strategy to ensure that they are on track to meet their retirement goals.

V Retirement Income Sources

There are several sources of retirement income that individuals can rely on to support their retirement lifestyle. Here are some of the most common sources of retirement income:

1. Social Security: Social Security is a government-administered program that provides retirement, disability, and survivor benefits. Workers and their employers pay into the Social Security system throughout their working years, and retirees can begin receiving benefits at age 62.

2. Pensions: Pensions are retirement plans that are typically provided by employers. They provide a guaranteed income stream for retirees based on factors such as years of service, salary, and age at retirement.

3. Retirement Savings: Retirement savings, such as 401(k) and IRA accounts, are a common source of retirement income. These accounts allow individuals to save and invest for retirement on a tax-advantaged basis.

4. Annuities: An annuity is an insurance product that provides a guaranteed income stream for a specified period of time or for the rest of an individual's life.

5. Real Estate: Real estate investments, such as rental properties or income-producing properties, can provide a source of retirement income.

6. Part-time work: Some retirees choose to work part-time during retirement to supplement their retirement income.

It's important for individuals to understand their sources of retirement income and how they can best utilize them to support their retirement lifestyle. For example, individuals may want to consider delaying Social Security benefits to maximize their monthly benefit, or they may want to structure their retirement savings withdrawals in a tax-efficient manner to minimize taxes. Consulting with a financial advisor can be helpful in developing a retirement income plan that takes into account an individual's unique circumstances and goals.

Maximizing retirement income often involves optimizing Social Security benefits and creating a sustainable withdrawal strategy for retirement savings. Here are some key considerations for each:

1. Optimizing Social Security Benefits: Social Security benefits can make up a significant portion of retirement income, so it's important to understand how to maximize these benefits. Some strategies include:

2. Delaying benefits: Individuals can receive Social Security benefits as early as age 62, but delaying benefits can increase the monthly benefit amount. For example, someone who delays benefits until age 70 can receive up to 132% of their full retirement age benefit amount.

3. Coordinating spousal benefits: Married couples may be able to optimize their benefits by coordinating when each spouse begins to receive benefits. For example, one spouse could delay benefits while the other begins to receive benefits, allowing the delayed benefits to grow while still receiving some income.

4. Maximizing survivor benefits: If one spouse passes away, the surviving spouse may be eligible for survivor benefits. Maximizing the primary earner's benefits can ensure that the surviving spouse receives the highest possible benefits.

5. Creating a Sustainable Withdrawal Strategy: Retirement savings can also play a key role in retirement income, and it's important to create a sustainable withdrawal strategy to ensure that these savings last throughout retirement. Some strategies include:

6. Following the 4% rule: The 4% rule suggests that retirees can withdraw 4% of their retirement savings in the first year of retirement, then adjust that amount each year for inflation. This can help ensure that retirees don't withdraw too much too quickly and run out of savings.

7. Considering tax implications: The way retirement savings are withdrawn can impact taxes. For example, withdrawing from traditional retirement accounts can increase taxable income, while withdrawing from Roth accounts can be tax-free.

8. Balancing investment risk: Retirees may want to consider a mix of investments that balances growth potential with downside risk. This can help ensure that retirement savings continue to grow while still protecting against market volatility.

By optimizing Social Security benefits and creating a sustainable withdrawal strategy for retirement savings, individuals can maximize their retirement income and help ensure a comfortable retirement. Working with a financial advisor can be helpful in developing a retirement income plan that takes into account an individual's unique circumstances and goals.

VI Healthcare Considerations

Healthcare costs can be a significant expense in retirement, and it's important to plan for these costs to ensure a comfortable retirement. Here are some key considerations for healthcare in retirement:

1. Medicare Coverage: Medicare is the primary healthcare coverage for individuals age 65 and older. It's important to understand the different parts of Medicare and their coverage to ensure that healthcare needs are covered.

2. Medicare Supplemental Coverage: While Medicare covers many healthcare expenses, it doesn't cover everything. Medicare supplemental coverage, such as Medigap policies or Medicare Advantage plans, can help cover additional healthcare expenses.
3. Long-Term Care: Long-term care, such as nursing home or in-home care, can be a significant expense in retirement. Long-term care insurance can help cover these expenses, but it's important to consider the costs and benefits of this coverage.
4. Health Savings Accounts: Health savings accounts (HSAs) are tax-advantaged accounts that can be used to pay for healthcare expenses. These accounts can be a valuable tool in retirement for covering healthcare expenses tax-free.
5. Overall Healthcare Costs: It's important to consider overall healthcare costs in retirement, including routine expenses such as premiums, deductibles, and co-payments, as well as unexpected expenses such as emergencies or chronic conditions. Estimating these costs and incorporating them into retirement planning can help ensure that healthcare expenses are adequately covered.

By considering healthcare costs and incorporating them into retirement planning, individuals can better prepare for healthcare expenses in retirement and ensure a comfortable retirement. Working with a financial advisor and healthcare professional can be helpful in developing a healthcare plan that meets an individual's unique needs and goals.

VII Estate Planning

Estate planning is an essential aspect of retirement planning. It involves creating a plan for how an individual's assets will be distributed after their death, as well as who will make important decisions regarding their healthcare and finances in the event they become incapacitated.

One of the most crucial components of estate planning is creating a will. A will is a legal document that outlines an individual's wishes for how their assets will be distributed after their death. It can also designate guardians for minor children and name an executor to oversee the distribution of assets.

Another important aspect of estate planning is assigning beneficiaries for retirement accounts, such as 401(k) or IRA accounts. This designation determines who will receive the assets in the account in the event of the account holder's death. It's important to review and update beneficiary designations regularly to ensure they align with an individual's wishes and current family situation.

Other estate planning tools include trusts, which can help minimize estate taxes and provide for the ongoing care of dependents, and powers of attorney, which designate individuals to make important healthcare and financial decisions in the event of incapacity.

By engaging in comprehensive estate planning, retirees can help ensure their assets are distributed according to their wishes and that their loved ones are taken care of after their death.

VIII. Monitoring Retirement Progress

Monitoring retirement progress is a critical aspect of retirement planning. It allows individuals to track their progress toward their retirement goals and make adjustments as needed to ensure they are on track for a comfortable retirement. Here are some steps to monitor retirement progress:

1. Review retirement goals: Regularly reviewing retirement goals can help individuals stay focused on their objectives and make necessary adjustments. It's essential to consider changes in personal circumstances or economic conditions that may impact retirement goals.

2. Track retirement savings: Tracking retirement savings can help individuals monitor progress toward their retirement goals. Reviewing account statements regularly and using retirement calculators can provide insight into whether retirement savings are on track to meet goals.

3. Adjust retirement savings strategies: If retirement savings are not on track to meet goals, it may be necessary to adjust savings strategies. This could involve increasing contributions to retirement accounts or exploring other investment options.

4. Review retirement income sources: Reviewing retirement income sources, such as Social Security and pensions, can help individuals estimate their retirement income and make necessary adjustments to ensure they will have enough income in retirement.

5. Reassess asset allocation: It's important to reassess asset allocation regularly to ensure it aligns with retirement goals and risk tolerance. Changes in personal circumstances or market conditions may require adjustments to asset allocation.

By monitoring retirement progress regularly, individuals can make necessary adjustments to their retirement planning strategies and ensure they are on track for a comfortable retirement.

The importance of regularly reviewing retirement goals and retirement savings plans

Regularly reviewing retirement goals and retirement savings plans is crucial to ensure individuals stay on track for a comfortable retirement. Here are some reasons why:

1. Life circumstances can change: Life is unpredictable, and circumstances can change in a moment's notice. For example, unexpected health issues, job loss, or a market downturn can impact retirement plans. Regularly reviewing retirement goals and savings plans can help individuals adjust their plans to account for changes in their lives.

2. Retirement goals may change: As individuals approach retirement, their goals may change. For example, they may decide they want to retire earlier or later than initially planned, travel more, or downsize their home. Regularly reviewing retirement goals can help individuals ensure their savings plan aligns with their current goals.

3. Economic conditions can change: Economic conditions can significantly impact retirement savings plans. For example, inflation or changes in interest rates can impact investment returns. Regularly reviewing savings plans and investment strategies can help individuals make adjustments to ensure their plan is still viable in changing economic conditions.

4. Retirement savings plans may not be sufficient: Without regular review, individuals may find they are not saving

enough to meet their retirement goals. Regularly reviewing retirement savings plans can help individuals identify gaps and make adjustments to ensure they have sufficient savings for retirement.

Overall, regularly reviewing retirement goals and savings plans can help individuals stay on track for a comfortable retirement. It allows for adjustments to be made as needed to account for life changes, changing goals, economic conditions, and savings shortfalls.

IX Conclusion

Retirement planning is crucial for ensuring a comfortable retirement. It requires setting clear retirement goals, determining retirement savings needs, managing investments, understanding retirement income sources, planning for healthcare costs, and estate planning. Regularly monitoring and adjusting retirement plans is also important to account for life changes, changing goals, economic conditions, and savings shortfalls. By planning early and regularly reviewing retirement plans, individuals can increase their chances of achieving a comfortable retirement and enjoying their golden years with financial security and peace of mind.

Remember this 10 Key take aways about Retirement Planning:

1. Retirement planning is important to ensure a comfortable retirement.
2. Setting clear retirement goals, including retirement age, lifestyle expectations, and financial needs, is essential for retirement planning.

3. Factors such as inflation, healthcare costs, and unexpected expenses should be considered when determining retirement savings needs.

4. There are various retirement savings options, including employer-sponsored plans, individual retirement accounts, and taxable investment accounts.

5. Retirement savings needs should be calculated, and the appropriate asset allocation should be determined based on retirement goals and risk tolerance.

6. Investment strategies such as diversification and asset allocation can help manage retirement investments.

7. Regular monitoring and adjustments of retirement plans are necessary to account for life changes, changing goals, economic conditions, and savings shortfalls.

8. Social Security, pensions, and retirement savings are common sources of retirement income.

9. Maximizing retirement income involves optimizing Social Security benefits and creating a sustainable withdrawal strategy for retirement savings.

10. Healthcare costs in retirement can be significant, and it is important to plan for them, including understanding how Medicare works and other healthcare options.

Absolutely. Starting retirement planning early is crucial for building a strong financial foundation for retirement. By starting early, individuals have more time to save and invest for retirement, and can take advantage of compounding interest to grow their retirement savings over time.

It's also important to seek professional advice if necessary. Financial advisors can provide guidance on retirement planning strategies, investment options, and other financial matters related to retirement. They can help individuals create a comprehensive retirement plan tailored to their unique needs and goals, and provide ongoing support to ensure that the plan stays on track.

In short, whether you are just starting your career or nearing retirement age, it's never too early or too late to start planning for retirement. By taking proactive steps and seeking professional advice when needed, you can increase your chances of achieving a comfortable retirement and enjoying financial security in your golden years.

CHAPTER 9

WEALTH PRESERVATION

I Introdcution

Wealth preservation refers to the strategies and methods used to protect an individual's accumulated assets and financial well-being from risks and threats that could diminish or deplete them. This can include measures to minimize taxes, manage risk, and ensure the transfer of wealth to future generations. In this chapter, we will examine various strategies for preserving wealth and securing a stable financial future.

Why wealth preservation is important

- Maintaining current lifestyle and financial security: Wealth preservation strategies can help individuals and families maintain their current standard of living, even in the face of unexpected financial challenges or economic downturns. By protecting their accumulated assets and minimizing risks, individuals can secure their financial future and avoid the negative consequences of financial instability.

- Passing on wealth to future generations: Effective wealth preservation strategies can help individuals pass on their accumulated assets to future generations in a tax-efficient manner. This can ensure that their loved ones are provided for and have the financial resources they need to achieve their goals and aspirations.

- Protecting against potential liabilities or risks: Wealth preservation can also protect individuals against potential liabilities or risks, such as legal judgments, lawsuits, or creditors. By implementing measures to protect their assets, individuals can safeguard their financial future and avoid the negative consequences of unforeseen events.

- Achieving long-term financial stability: Wealth preservation is critical for achieving long-term financial stability and security. By implementing effective wealth preservation strategies, individuals can create a solid foundation for their financial future and ensure that they have the resources they need to achieve their goals and aspirations.
- Providing for loved ones for generations to come: Ultimately, wealth preservation is about providing for loved ones for generations to come. By implementing effective wealth preservation strategies, individuals can secure their financial future and ensure that their loved ones are provided for, even after they are gone.

II Types of Wealth

Here's an overview of different types of wealth:

1. Financial wealth: This refers to assets that have monetary value, such as cash, stocks, bonds, real estate, and other investments.
2. Physical wealth: This refers to tangible assets that have value, such as property, art, jewelry, vehicles, and other physical possessions.
3. Intellectual wealth: This refers to intangible assets that have value, such as patents, copyrights, trademarks, and other forms of intellectual property.
4. Social wealth: This refers to the value that individuals or organizations derive from their relationships and networks, including social capital, reputation, and influence.
5. Spiritual wealth: This refers to the value that individuals derive from their sense of purpose, meaning, and connection to something larger than themselves.

6. Emotional wealth: This refers to the value that individuals derive from their relationships, experiences, and emotional well-being.

7. Environmental wealth: This refers to the value that individuals derive from the natural environment, including ecosystem services and the preservation of biodiversity.

The importance of identifying and protecting different types of wealth

Protecting different types of wealth is important because they can all contribute to an individual or family's overall financial well-being. Here are some examples:

1. Financial Wealth: This includes assets such as cash, investments, real estate, and other tangible assets. Protecting financial wealth involves ensuring that it is invested in a diversified portfolio and that adequate insurance coverage is in place.

2. Physical Wealth: This includes assets such as property, art, and other valuables. Protecting physical wealth involves implementing security measures, such as alarms and insurance coverage, to guard against theft, damage, or loss.

3. Intellectual Wealth: This includes assets such as patents, trademarks, copyrights, and other intellectual property. Protecting intellectual wealth involves registering and defending these assets to prevent others from using or profiting from them without permission.

4. Human Capital: This includes an individual's knowledge, skills, and abilities, which can be leveraged to generate income and create financial security. Protecting human capital involves investing in education and training, maintaining good health, and acquiring adequate disability and life insurance coverage.

It is important to identify and protect all types of wealth to ensure long-term financial stability and security.

III Wealth Preservation Strategies

There are various wealth preservation strategies that individuals and families can use to protect their wealth and ensure that it is passed on to future generations. Here are some common strategies:

1. Estate Planning: This involves creating a plan for the distribution of your assets upon your death. This may involve creating a will, setting up trusts, and assigning beneficiaries to your retirement accounts.

2. Asset Protection: This strategy involves protecting your assets from potential lawsuits or creditors. This may involve setting up a limited liability company (LLC) or a trust to hold your assets.

3. Insurance: Insurance can be an important tool for protecting your wealth, particularly against unforeseen events such as accidents, illness, or natural disasters. Types of insurance to consider include life insurance, disability insurance, and long-term care insurance.

4. Tax Planning: By understanding the tax implications of your financial decisions, you can reduce your tax burden and preserve your wealth. This may involve strategies such as investing in tax-advantaged accounts, making charitable donations, or utilizing gifting strategies.

5. Diversification: Diversifying your investments can help protect your wealth against market fluctuations and economic

downturns. This may involve investing in a variety of asset classes, such as stocks, bonds, real estate, and commodities.

6. Continuity Planning: Continuity planning involves creating a plan for the continuity of your business or other assets in the event of your death or incapacitation. This may involve identifying a successor or creating a plan for the sale of your business.

7. Education and Communication: Educating your heirs about financial management and communicating your wealth preservation strategies to them can help ensure that your wealth is managed and preserved according to your wishes.

These strategies can be used in various combinations to create a comprehensive wealth preservation plan. It is important to work with a financial advisor or attorney who specializes in wealth management to create a plan that is tailored to your individual needs and goals.

By utilizing these wealth preservation strategies, you can help ensure that your assets are protected and passed on to future generations in a tax-efficient and effective manner.

key components of estate planning (wills, trusts, power of attorney, etc.)

Estate planning is an essential aspect of wealth preservation, and it involves creating a plan for the distribution of assets after death. The following are some key components of estate planning:

1. Will: A will is a legal document that outlines how a person's assets will be distributed after their death. It is important to

have a will in place, regardless of the amount of wealth, to ensure that the individual's wishes are carried out.

2. Trusts: Trusts are legal arrangements in which a trustee holds and manages assets on behalf of beneficiaries. There are different types of trusts, such as revocable and irrevocable trusts, and they can be used to minimize estate taxes, protect assets from creditors, and provide for beneficiaries with specific needs.

3. Power of attorney: A power of attorney is a legal document that designates an individual to make financial and legal decisions on behalf of the person who created the document. This can be important if the individual becomes incapacitated or unable to make decisions on their own.

4. Beneficiary designations: Beneficiary designations are instructions that specify who should receive certain assets, such as retirement accounts or life insurance policies, after the individual's death. It is important to keep beneficiary designations up-to-date and consistent with the overall estate plan.

5. Letter of instruction: A letter of instruction is a non-legal document that outlines the individual's wishes regarding their funeral, burial or cremation, and any other specific requests. While not legally binding, it can provide guidance to loved ones during a difficult time.

These components of estate planning can help ensure that an individual's assets are distributed according to their wishes and can also help minimize taxes, protect assets from creditors, and provide for loved ones.

How estate planning can help ensure that wealth is passed onto future generations

Estate planning is an essential part of wealth preservation as it can help ensure that wealth is passed on to future generations in a tax-efficient and organized manner. Without proper estate planning, the distribution of wealth can become complicated and potentially result in legal disputes or financial losses.

One key component of estate planning is creating a will, which outlines how assets will be distributed after an individual's death. Wills can be simple or complex, depending on the size and complexity of the estate. They can also be updated as circumstances change, such as when new assets are acquired or when beneficiaries need to be added or removed.

Trusts are another important tool in estate planning. They are legal entities that hold and manage assets for the benefit of beneficiaries. Trusts can provide greater flexibility and control over the distribution of assets, as well as provide protection from creditors and lawsuits.

Powers of attorney are also a crucial part of estate planning. They allow individuals to appoint someone to make financial and legal decisions on their behalf in the event they become incapacitated.

Overall, estate planning can help ensure that wealth is passed on to future generations in a way that aligns with an individual's wishes and minimizes the tax burden on their heirs.

V Asset Protection

Asset protection refers to the set of legal strategies and techniques used to protect an individual's wealth and assets from potential threats such as lawsuits, creditors, or other financial risks. These strategies can include the use of legal entities like trusts, limited liability companies (LLCs), and family limited partnerships, as well as insurance policies and other risk management tools.

Asset protection can help to safeguard an individual's assets and wealth by limiting the amount of financial exposure they have to potential risks. By implementing these strategies, individuals can help to protect their personal and business assets, and ensure that they are able to maintain their financial security over the long term.

Some common asset protection strategies include:

1. Incorporating a business or forming an LLC to limit personal liability
2. Establishing a trust to hold assets and protect them from potential creditors
3. Transferring ownership of assets to family members or other trusted individuals
4. Purchasing liability insurance to protect against potential legal claims
5. Utilizing retirement accounts and other tax-advantaged vehicles to shelter assets from taxes and potential legal claims

Overall, asset protection is an important component of wealth preservation, as it can help to safeguard an individual's financial security and ensure that their assets are protected from potential threats. By working with a financial advisor or other professional, individuals can develop a comprehensive asset protection strategy that meets their unique needs and goals.

Overview of different asset protection strategies (limited liability companies, asset protection trusts, etc.)

There are various asset protection strategies that can be used to safeguard wealth, some of which are:

1. Limited liability companies (LLCs): Setting up an LLC can provide liability protection for business owners by separating their personal assets from their business assets. This can help protect personal assets from lawsuits and other legal actions taken against the business.

2. Asset protection trusts: These trusts are specifically designed to protect assets from creditors and lawsuits. They work by placing assets into a trust, which is managed by a trustee. The trust can be set up so that the assets are protected from creditors while still allowing the beneficiary to access the assets for their own use.

3. Family limited partnerships (FLPs): FLPs are partnerships that are typically set up by family members for the purpose of managing and protecting family assets. They can be used to shield assets from creditors, reduce estate taxes, and provide a way for family members to pass assets on to future generations.

4. Homestead exemptions: Homestead exemptions are laws that protect a portion of a person's home equity from creditors in the event of a bankruptcy or other legal action. The amount of the exemption varies by state.

5. Insurance: Insurance can be used as an asset protection strategy by providing coverage for potential liability or loss of assets. This can include liability insurance for businesses, malpractice insurance for professionals, and umbrella policies for individuals.

6. Offshore accounts and trusts: Some individuals use offshore accounts and trusts to protect their assets from legal action or seizure. While this strategy can be effective, it is important to seek professional advice and ensure that all legal and tax requirements are met.

How asset protection can be integrated into an overall wealth preservation plan

Asset protection is an important component of wealth preservation, and it can be integrated into an overall plan that also includes estate planning and insurance. One approach to asset protection is to hold assets in a way that limits exposure to liability. This can involve using limited liability companies or family limited partnerships to hold assets, which can help protect those assets from creditors or legal claims.

Another approach to asset protection is to use asset protection trusts, which are specifically designed to shield assets from creditors. These trusts can be established in jurisdictions that have favorable laws for asset protection, such as Delaware, Nevada, or South Dakota. However, it's important to work with an experienced attorney to ensure that these trusts are set up correctly and in compliance with applicable laws.

It's also important to note that while asset protection strategies can help safeguard assets, they are not foolproof. Creditors may still be able to access assets held in certain types of trusts or through certain types of entities, and legal challenges to asset protection arrangements are not uncommon. Therefore, it's important to work with a professional to design a comprehensive wealth preservation plan that takes into account all relevant factors and risks.

VI Insurance

Insurance is a means of transferring risk from an individual to an insurance company in exchange for a premium payment. It is an important component of wealth preservation as it helps protect individuals and their assets from unexpected events or losses that could negatively impact their financial stability.

There are various types of insurance, including life insurance, disability insurance, long-term care insurance, property and casualty insurance, and liability insurance. Each type of insurance offers specific coverage and benefits to help protect different aspects of an individual's wealth.

Life insurance can provide financial support to loved ones in the event of the policyholder's death, while disability insurance can provide income replacement in the event of a disability that prevents the policyholder from working. Long-term care insurance can help cover the costs of nursing home care or in-home care in the event of a prolonged illness or disability.

Property and casualty insurance, such as homeowners insurance or auto insurance, can help protect physical assets from unexpected damage or loss, while liability insurance can protect individuals from legal claims or lawsuits that may arise from accidents or other incidents.

When considering insurance as a wealth preservation strategy, it's important to carefully evaluate different policies and providers to ensure they meet individual needs and budget.

Regularly reviewing and updating insurance coverage is also important to ensure it remains adequate and up-to-date as circumstances change.

different types of insurance (life insurance, disability insurance, long-term care insurance, etc.) and their role in wealth preservation

Insurance is a crucial component of wealth preservation, as it can provide a safety net against unexpected events that could jeopardize an individual's financial well-being. Here are some key points to consider:

1. Life insurance: This type of insurance provides a lump-sum payment to beneficiaries upon the policyholder's death. It can be used to replace lost income, pay off debts, or provide for dependents.
2. Disability insurance: This insurance provides income replacement in the event that an individual becomes unable to work due to injury or illness. It can help protect against the loss of income and help cover expenses related to the disability.
3. Long-term care insurance: This insurance can help cover the costs of long-term care, such as nursing home care, home health care, and assisted living. It can help protect against the high costs of long-term care, which can quickly deplete an individual's savings.
4. Property and casualty insurance: This type of insurance includes homeowners insurance, auto insurance, and liability insurance. It can help protect against financial losses due to property damage, theft, or lawsuits.

5. Health insurance: Health insurance is important for protecting against the high costs of medical care. It can help cover expenses related to illness or injury, including hospitalizations, surgeries, and prescription drugs.

Overall, insurance can play a crucial role in protecting an individual's wealth by providing a safety net against unexpected events. It is important to carefully consider the different types of insurance available and how they can be integrated into an overall wealth preservation plan.

VII Tax Planning

Tax planning is an essential aspect of wealth preservation as it helps individuals and families minimize tax liabilities and preserve more of their wealth. This involves understanding different tax laws and regulations and structuring finances and investments in a tax-efficient manner.

Key points to consider in tax planning for wealth preservation include:

1. Understanding the tax implications of different types of income, such as earned income, capital gains, and dividends.
2. Knowing the different tax brackets and rates and how they apply to different types of income and investments.
3. Identifying tax deductions and credits that can be used to reduce tax liabilities.
4. Considering tax-deferred or tax-free investment options, such as retirement accounts and municipal bonds.
5. Staying up-to-date on changes to tax laws and regulations and adjusting planning strategies as needed.

By incorporating tax planning into an overall wealth preservation plan, individuals and families can minimize tax liabilities and preserve more of their wealth for future generations.

different tax planning strategies (gift tax, estate tax, etc.) and how they can be used to preserve wealth

Here are some key points on tax planning strategies for wealth preservation:

1. Gift Tax Planning: This involves gifting assets to beneficiaries during the individual's lifetime to reduce the amount of the individual's taxable estate. Gifts up to a certain amount each year are exempt from gift taxes, and gifts over that amount can be subject to taxes.

2. Estate Tax Planning: This involves creating an estate plan that reduces or eliminates the impact of estate taxes on the individual's assets after their death. Strategies may include setting up trusts or making gifts to beneficiaries during the individual's lifetime.

3. Charitable Giving: Charitable giving can provide significant tax benefits while also supporting causes that are important to the individual. Charitable donations can reduce taxable income and estate taxes.

4. Retirement Account Planning: Careful planning of retirement accounts, such as 401(k)s and IRAs, can help reduce the impact of taxes on retirement savings. This may include strategies such as converting traditional retirement accounts to Roth accounts.

5. Business Succession Planning: For individuals who own businesses, business succession planning can help ensure

that the business remains viable and the individual's wealth is protected. This may include strategies such as transferring ownership to family members or key employees, or setting up a buy-sell agreement.

By implementing these tax planning strategies, individuals can help preserve their wealth and reduce the impact of taxes on their assets. It is important to work with a qualified financial advisor or tax professional to develop a tax planning strategy that is tailored to their specific circumstances.

VIII Charitable Giving

Charitable giving refers to the act of donating money or assets to charitable organizations, causes, or individuals in need. Charitable giving can be a valuable wealth preservation strategy for several reasons. First, it can help reduce estate taxes by reducing the size of the estate. Second, it can provide an opportunity to support causes or organizations that align with the individual's values and beliefs. Finally, charitable giving can provide a sense of fulfillment and purpose in knowing that one's wealth is being used to make a positive impact in the world.

There are several ways to engage in charitable giving as a wealth preservation strategy. One common approach is to establish a charitable trust or foundation, which can provide tax benefits while allowing the donor to retain some control over how their funds are used. Charitable remainder trusts and charitable lead trusts are two examples of trusts that can be used for charitable giving.

Another approach to charitable giving is to make direct donations to charitable organizations or causes. Many organizations offer tax deductions for charitable donations, which can help reduce the donor's tax burden while supporting a worthy cause.

Overall, charitable giving can be a valuable wealth preservation strategy for those looking to make a positive impact with their wealth while also reducing their tax liability.

Different charitable giving strategies (charitable trusts, donor-advised funds, etc.) and their benefits

Charitable giving can be an effective wealth preservation strategy that provides benefits to both the giver and the recipient. There are several charitable giving strategies that can be utilized:

1. Charitable Trusts: These are trusts that allow the donor to make a charitable gift while still retaining some control over the assets. There are two main types of charitable trusts: charitable remainder trusts and charitable lead trusts. Charitable remainder trusts provide the donor with income for a set number of years, after which the assets are transferred to a charity. Charitable lead trusts provide income to a charity for a set number of years, after which the assets are returned to the donor or their beneficiaries.

2. Donor-Advised Funds: These are funds that are set up by a donor at a community foundation or other financial institution. The donor contributes assets to the fund and can then recommend grants to specific charities over time. Donor-advised funds provide a flexible and tax-efficient way for donors to support charitable causes.

3. Private Foundations: Private foundations are non-profit organizations that are established by individuals or families to support charitable causes. Private foundations can provide a high degree of control over the use of charitable assets, but they also require significant administrative and legal resources.

Overall, charitable giving can provide significant tax benefits while also allowing donors to support causes that are important to them. By incorporating charitable giving into a wealth preservation plan, individuals can help ensure that their wealth has a positive impact on society while also benefiting their families and future generations.

VIII Conclusion

Yes, it is important for individuals to prioritize wealth preservation and take steps towards protecting their assets and passing them on to future generations. By implementing strategies such as estate planning, asset protection, insurance, tax planning, and charitable giving, individuals can create a comprehensive wealth preservation plan that addresses all aspects of their financial situation. It is also important to work with professionals, such as financial advisors, attorneys, and accountants, to ensure that the wealth preservation plan is tailored to the individual's unique needs and goals.

Effective wealth preservation strategies can be an important component of achieving financial success and leaving a lasting legacy for future generations. To ensure that your wealth is protected and passed on to your heirs in the most efficient and effective manner possible, it is important to take a holistic approach to wealth preservation. This may include a combination of estate planning, asset protection, insurance, tax planning, and charitable giving strategies, tailored to your unique financial situation and goals.

It is also important to regularly review and update your wealth preservation plan as your circumstances and financial goals evolve over time. Seeking professional advice from an experienced financial planner or estate planning attorney can be a valuable step in developing and implementing an effective wealth preservation plan.

Ultimately, the key to achieving financial success and preserving your wealth is to start early, stay informed, and be proactive in taking the necessary steps to protect and grow your assets over time. With a clear understanding of the different wealth preservation strategies available, and a commitment to implementing them effectively, you can help ensure that your hard-earned wealth will continue to benefit you and your loved ones for generations to come.

CHAPTER 10

I. GIVING BACK: THE IMPORTANCE OF PHILANTHROPY AND GIVING BACK, & STRATEGIES FOR DOING SO EFFECTIVELY

Philanthropy and giving back refer to the act of donating time, resources, or money to charitable causes or organizations that benefit society. These acts of generosity play an important role in promoting positive change and addressing social issues such as poverty, healthcare, education, and the environment. In this chapter, we will explore the importance of philanthropy and discuss strategies for giving back effectively.

II The Benefits of Philanthropy

Philanthropy has several benefits. Firstly, it provides a sense of personal fulfillment as individuals are able to contribute to causes that align with their values and beliefs. Additionally, philanthropy has a positive impact on the community, addressing societal issues and supporting organizations that provide critical services. Philanthropy can also result in tax benefits, such as tax deductions for donations made to qualified charities. Furthermore, philanthropy can enhance an individual's reputation and influence within their community.

1. Personal fulfillment: Giving back through philanthropy can provide a sense of personal fulfillment and satisfaction, as it allows individuals to make a positive impact on the world around them.

2. Community impact: Philanthropy can help support important causes and organizations, such as charities, non-profits, and community initiatives. By donating time, money, or resources, individuals can help make a difference in the lives of others and improve their communities.

3. Tax benefits: Philanthropic giving can also provide tax benefits, as donations to qualified organizations are often

tax-deductible. This can help individuals reduce their tax burden while supporting causes they care about.

4. Networking opportunities: Philanthropy can also provide networking opportunities, as individuals can connect with like-minded individuals and organizations who share their values and interests.

5. Legacy building: Philanthropy can help individuals leave a lasting impact and build a positive legacy, as their contributions can continue to benefit their communities and causes for years to come.

III Types of Philanthropic Giving

Donating money: This is one of the most common forms of philanthropy. It involves giving financial resources to support charitable organizations or causes.

Volunteering time: This involves giving one's time and expertise to help organizations achieve their mission. This can include activities such as mentoring, serving on a board, or providing pro bono services.

Donating goods and services: This involves giving tangible items or services that can be used by charitable organizations to support their activities. This can include donations of clothing, food, or supplies, or providing services such as legal or accounting services.

Corporate philanthropy: This involves companies giving back to the community through charitable donations, employee volunteer programs, or other initiatives.

Individual philanthropy: This involves individuals giving back to the community through charitable donations, volunteering, or other activities.

IV Strategies for Effective Giving

Effective giving involves being strategic and intentional about how one donates time, money, and resources to charitable causes. Here are some strategies that can help individuals give more effectively:

1. Research charities: Before donating to a charity, it is important to research and understand its mission, impact, and financial management practices. Online resources such as Charity Navigator and GuideStar provide information on nonprofit organizations' financial health, accountability, and transparency.

2. Set giving goals: Establishing clear giving goals can help individuals identify the causes they are most passionate about and focus their philanthropic efforts in a way that aligns with their values and priorities.

3. Create a giving plan: A giving plan can help individuals budget their giving, determine how much they can afford to give, and allocate their resources to maximize impact. The plan can include factors such as the causes and organizations to support, the type and amount of donations, and a timeline for giving.

4. Consider impact and effectiveness: When deciding where to donate, individuals should consider the potential impact of their donations and the effectiveness of the organizations they support. Evaluating the success of past projects, measuring

outcomes, and understanding how donations will be used can help individuals make informed decisions about where to give.

5. Monitor impact: Regularly monitoring the impact of donations can help individuals ensure that their giving is making a difference and identify opportunities to adjust their philanthropic strategies as needed.

By following these strategies, individuals can make the most of their philanthropic efforts and have a greater impact on the causes they care about.

V Maximizing the Impact of Donations

Giving to high-impact charities: Donating to charities that have a proven track record of making a positive impact in their respective areas is one way to maximize the impact of donations. It is important to do research on charities before making donations to ensure that they are effective and use donations efficiently.

Leveraging matching gifts: Many companies and employers offer matching gift programs, where they match their employees' charitable contributions up to a certain amount. This is a great way to increase the impact of donations without spending additional funds.

Creating a giving circle: A giving circle is a group of individuals who pool their money and resources together to make donations to charities. This approach allows individuals to make a bigger impact than they would on their own, and it also fosters a sense of community and collaboration around philanthropy.

In-kind donations: Donating goods and services can be an effective way to maximize the impact of donations. For example, donating gently used clothing or furniture to a charity can provide much-needed resources for individuals and families in need.

VI Philanthropy and Personal Finance

Philanthropy can play an important role in personal finance and financial planning. It is essential to consider philanthropy as part of the overall financial plan to ensure that giving goals align with other financial priorities and objectives.

One important consideration is creating a philanthropic budget, which involves setting aside a certain amount of money each year for charitable giving. This can be done by setting a percentage of income or a fixed dollar amount. It is important to ensure that the philanthropic budget does not interfere with other financial obligations, such as saving for retirement or paying off debt.

Another important aspect is maximizing tax benefits. Charitable contributions are tax-deductible, so it is essential to understand the tax implications of giving. Tax benefits can be maximized by giving appreciated assets, such as stocks or real estate, instead of cash. This can result in significant tax savings, as donors can avoid capital gains taxes on the appreciated assets.

It is also important to consider the long-term impact of philanthropy on personal finance.

Philanthropic giving can help create a legacy and ensure that values and beliefs are passed down through future generations.

It is essential to involve family members in the philanthropic process and create a plan that aligns with the family's values and goals. This can help ensure that philanthropy is a sustainable and meaningful part of the family's financial plan.

- Creating a philanthropic budget can help individuals make charitable giving a regular and sustainable part of their financial plan.
- Maximizing tax benefits such as deductions or credits can help individuals make the most of their charitable donations.

VII Giving as a Family

1. Philanthropy can be a valuable way for families to bond and work together towards a shared goal of making a positive impact in their community or the world.
2. Engaging children in philanthropic activities can help teach important values like empathy, generosity, and social responsibility.

   Giving as a family can also create a legacy of giving that extends beyond an individual's lifetime and can have a lasting impact on future generations.

3. When involving children in philanthropy, it's important to consider their age and interests, and to make sure the activities are engaging and meaningful for them.
4. Family giving can take many forms, from volunteering together to establishing a family foundation or donor-advised fund to support causes that are important to the family.

VIII Corporate Philanthropy

Corporate philanthropy refers to a company's charitable contributions to social causes, organizations, and initiatives. It is an effective way for businesses to give back to society while also improving their reputation, employee morale, and customer loyalty. Some of the common strategies for effective corporate giving include aligning giving with the company's mission and values, creating partnerships with nonprofit organizations, and engaging employees in volunteer opportunities. Additionally, measuring the impact of corporate philanthropy can help ensure that resources are being directed towards the most effective and impactful causes.

1. Corporate philanthropy can take many different forms, including charitable donations, volunteer work, cause-related marketing, and corporate social responsibility initiatives.

2. Many companies engage in corporate philanthropy as a way to build their brand, enhance their reputation, and foster goodwill among customers, employees, and other stakeholders.

3. Corporate philanthropy can have a positive impact on communities and society at large, providing support for causes such as education, healthcare, the environment, and social justice.

4. Corporate philanthropy can also provide benefits for businesses themselves, such as tax breaks and positive public relations.

5. Some critics argue that corporate philanthropy can be a form of "greenwashing" or a way for companies to distract from unethical business practices or harmful environmental impact.

6. To be effective, corporate philanthropy should be aligned with a company's core values and mission, and should be integrated into the company's overall business strategy.

Corporate philanthropy can be a powerful tool for employee engagement and retention, as employees are often motivated by the opportunity to give back to their communities and feel proud of their company's social impact.

7. The rise of social media and other digital platforms has made it easier for companies to promote their philanthropic activities and engage with customers and other stakeholders around shared values and causes.

8. Many companies are now moving beyond traditional forms of corporate philanthropy and engaging in more innovative approaches, such as impact investing, social entrepreneurship, and shared value creation.

9. Overall, corporate philanthropy can be a valuable way for companies to make a positive impact on society while also benefiting their own bottom line and reputation. However, it is important for companies to approach philanthropy with authenticity and a genuine commitment to making a difference, rather than simply as a marketing or public relations tactic.

In conclusion, giving back through philanthropy is a powerful way to make a positive impact on society and improve the lives of those in need.

Therefore, it is important to prioritize giving back in both personal and professional life. This can be done by finding causes and organizations that align with individual or organizational values, volunteering time and expertise, making charitable donations, and incorporating social responsibility into business practices. By taking action and making philanthropy a priority, individuals and businesses can make a positive difference in the world while also experiencing personal and professional growth and fulfillment.

Thank you for taking the time to read "Wealthyfull." I hope this book has provided you with valuable insights into the concept of financial freedom and its significance in your life. Remember that true happiness and fulfillment come not only from building wealth for yourself but also from giving back to society. By creating wealth that benefits not only yourself but also society as a whole, you can experience a greater sense of purpose and satisfaction. Once again, thank you for your time and I wish you all the best on your journey to financial freedom.

– Dr R Senthil MBA.,Ph.D.,CFP.,AIII

9 789356 484078